SEA

U.S.S.R.

Samsun

Trabzon Rize Artvin Kars

Ağri

Erzincan Erzurum Doğubayazit

R. Euphrates

Sivas

Ahlat

Lake Van

Bingöl

Van

Elaziğ

Akhtamar
Island

Malatya

Siirt

Nemrut
Dağ Diyarbakir R. Tigris Hakkari

Adiyaman

ayseri

Mardin

oprakkale Gaziantep Urfa IRAQ

Issus

IRAN

İskenderun

N

Antakya

W E

SYRIA

S

R. Euphrates

R. Tigris

Kilometres

0   100   200

TURKEY

A TIMELESS BRIDGE

TURKEY

A TIMELESS BRIDGE

PETER HOLMES

ACKNOWLEDGEMENTS

I would like to express thanks to the following for permission to publish their photographs: J. Allan Cash for the photographs on pages 152, 161 (bottom) and 176; Hugh Bodington for that on page 180 (top); Sami Güner for those on pages 56, 57, 62, 63 and 64; Mark Moody-Stuart for those on pages 77 (top), 86, 177 and 179; Sidney and Hilary Nowill for those on pages 76 (top), 82, 97, 118 and 119; Gavan Sellers for those on pages 70, 105, 120 (bottom) and 173 (top); and my wife Judy for those on pages 66 and 68.

The remaining photographs in this book are among the thousands I have taken in Turkey over the past fifteen years. These are held by the J. Allan Cash Photo Library in London.

In my travels around Turkey and in my research for this book I was helped by many people, too numerous to mention individually. But I would especially like to thank Chris Fay and Mark Moody-Stuart, whose enthusiasm has kept the project on track; and the members of The Shell Company of Turkey Ltd. and Turkse Shell N.V. who have assisted me in so many ways.

Special mention should be made of Dr. Alastair Lamb of Hertford, England, whose encyclopaedic historical scholarship was put at my disposal and was of the greatest value in formulating the essay.

The design of this book owes much to Laurence Bradbury. Barbara Baylis assisted with the book's preparation; Freddie Mansfield and his staff with photographic organisation; and Gillian Thorn with laborious proof-reading. Sayhan Bilbaşar has provided much expertise.

Finally, I would like to thank The Shell Company of Turkey Ltd., without whose sponsorship this book would not have been possible.

First published in Turkey in 1988
by The Shell Company of Turkey Limited.

Copyright in the text and illustrations © Peter Holmes 1988

Design: Laurence Bradbury

Printed and bound by Apa Ofset Basimevi, Istanbul, Turkey

ISBN 0.9513165.0.8

Half title: 17th century Iznik Jug.

Frontispiece: Kemal Atatürk ascending the Kocatepe Hill, on the dawn of the Great Offensive during the Turkish Independence War.

Opposite: Painting of the Golden Horn at Istanbul by the author's grandfather, Charles Fenwick Holmes.

Front Cover: The theatre at Pergamum.

Back Cover: The Galata Tower, Istanbul.

CONTENTS

FOREWORD

My interest in Turkey began when I was a small boy. We lived in Budapest, but I was aware that my father looked back to the days before the First World War with much nostalgia; for he had been born and had grown up in Istanbul. The family albums abounded with photographs of life as it had been in Turkey at the turn of the century.

The family connection with Turkey goes back to the 1840's. My great-grandfather, Sir William Richard Holmes (1822-1882), worked in the British Levant Consular Service. His postings included Erzurum (1841-1845), Samsun (1846), Batum (1846-1852), Diyarbakir (1852-1854), Monastir (1854-1860) and Bosna-Serai (1860-1877). Thus he lived in many of the more remote but most beautiful parts of Turkey and the Ottoman Empire. He had eight children, and the second of these was my grandfather, Charles Fenwick Holmes (1852-1935). Born in Erzurum, he lived in Turkey all his working life. He loved Turkey, as can be seen in the many paintings he left of the country. His son was my father, Gerald Hugh Holmes (1896-1950).

Over the years I have visited Turkey many times. It is a fascinating country to travel in, for it combines superb and extremely varied scenery, a wealth of archaeology and history, a favourable climate, and delicious and wholesome food, with a people whose qualities are easy to admire and who are renowned for their hospitality.

I have long visualised Turkey as the link between Asia and Europe. Politically, as we shall see in the essay, this was not always the case. Often invaders from the East found the Anatolian Peninsula the limit of their expansion: for them it was more of a barrier. But this was not true of the Persians, the Macedonians, the Romans, the Byzantines and the Ottomans; for the Ottomans especially Anatolia was a bridge on their march to Empire.

If you put aside politics, however, and look to trade and commodities, the flow of ideas, civilisation itself, all these found Anatolia a bridge linking East and West. Hence the title of this book.

Turkey is a wondrous country. If this book captures in some small measure the feeling of history and beauty that envelops the traveller, it will have served its purpose.

PETER HOLMES,
LONDON, 1988

Opposite: Byzantine Church above the chasm at Kanytelis, south coast.

CHRONOLOGY

Date	Civilisation	Sites	Events
To c.7500 BC	Paleolithic (Old Stone Age)	Hunting and early agriculture	Trade in obsidian from 8000 BC.
c.6500 BC	Neolithic (New Stone Age)	Çatal Hüyük	World's first landscape painting (of volcano erupting). Pottery.
c.5500-4500 BC	Chalcolithic	Hacilar near Burdur	First walled towns.
c.4500-2500 BC		Troy 1, 3500-3000 BC	Quiescent period, some continuing migrations.
c.2500-1800 BC	Bronze Age-Hatti	Alaca Hüyük	Rule over much of Anatolia.
c.1800-1200 BC	Late Bronze Age-Hittite	Hattusas	Highly developed Empire over Anatolia and Syria.
		Troy VI	Trojan War, c.1250 BC.
c.1200-1100 BC			Invasion by 'Peoples of the Sea'.
c.900-600 BC	Urartian	Van	Impressive public works.
c.900-550 BC	Phrygian	Gordium	King Midas. Huge burial mounds.
c.700-550 BC	Lydian	Sardis	King Croesus. Invention of coinage. Sardis captured by Persians, 546 BC.
c.700-550 BC	Lycian	Xanthus	Elaborate rock tombs.
c.1150-550 C	Ionians	Miletus, Priene and others	Distinct and brilliant culture.
c.550-334 BC	Persian	(Iran)	Anatolia part of first World Empire. Highly developed road system. 334 BC-Alexander defeats Darius III.
334-133 BC	Hellenistic	Ephesus, Miletus and others	Flowering of Aegean Hellenistic culture.
133 BC-330 AD	Roman	Ephesus, Smyrna, Antioch	Asiatic Province of Roman Empire.
330-1453 AD	Byzantine	Constantinople	330-new capital of Roman Empire. 1071-battle of Manzikert. 1453-fall of Constantinople.
1071-1281 AD	Seljuk	Konya	1071-battle of Manzikert gives Seljuks control of Anatolia. 1243-Seljuks defeated by Mongols, become vassal state. Rise of independent principalities or beyliks.
1281-1922 AD	Ottoman	Bursa, Edirne, Constantinople	1326-Bursa captured and made capital. c.1365-Edirne becomes capital. 1402-Timur defeats Beyazit. 1453-capture of Constantinople. 1550-1700-greatest extent of Ottoman Empire.
1922-present	Turkish Republic	Ankara	Genius of Atatürk, 1881-1936.

The above chronology ignores the many invasions which were either repulsed or which created no permanent new order. These invaders include the Sassanians, the Arabs, the Crusaders, the Mongols, the Timurids and many others.

ESSAY

The Turks, in their origins, belong to a group of peoples from Central Asia who speak languages of the Uralo Altaic family. The earliest examples of varieties of Turkish in the written form are to be found in stone inscriptions dating to the 7th century AD from Siberia and Mongolia; but the history of Turkish speakers goes back much further than this. It may be that the Hsiung-nu of the Chinese Han Dynasty records (c. 200 BC) were Turkish in this sense.

History reveals that over the last 2000 years or so there have been numerous Turkish empires or other major political structures. During most of the 7th, 8th and 9th centuries AD, for instance, the greater part of the vast Central Asian landmass separating Europe from the borders of China was dominated by Turkish tribes who for a while were united into a single empire (The Göktürk Empire in modern Turkish terminology) which, at its height, was among the most powerful states in the early Medieval world, T'ang Dynasty China, the Umayyad Caliphate, the Byzantine Empire and the Carolingian Empire not excepted. We know of it mainly from external sources, from the Chinese who saw it as a threat to their security beyond the Great Wall, from the Byzantines who found it convenient to enter into diplomatic relations with it including imperial marriage alliances, and from the works of a number of travellers and historians writing in Arabic.

The last years of the 14th century AD witnessed another example of Turkish empire-building skills in the creation of the empire of Timur (or Tamerlane) which embraced much of the western part of Central Asia along with Iran and the eastern Mediterranean borderlands. The Timurid Empire was relatively short-lived. During its opening years, however, it was to have a devastating effect on Turkish history. In the longer term the Timurid Empire was to give birth to an offspring in the shape of the Moghul Empire in India which was established by Timur's great-great-grandson Babur in the early 16th century, building on the foundations of a process of Turkish invasion and conquest in northern India going back to the first incursions of Mahmud of Ghazni in the late 10th century AD.

Of all the empires created by the Turks (and by peoples of Central or Inner Asian origin related to them on linguistic grounds like the Mongols and, more remotely, the Tungus of whom the Manchus are perhaps the best known), that of the Ottoman Turks out of which modern Turkey emerged after World War I, was in some ways the most remarkable. Its duration, from its rather obscure beginnings in the late 13th century AD to the formal proclamation of the Turkish Republic in 1923, was over 600 years, far longer than the life of the Moghuls in India. It proved for much of its history extraordinarily capable of meeting a wide range of challenges. By the middle of the 17th century the Ottoman Turks were probably as effective a body politic as any in either Asia or Europe. Indeed, it still looked to some contemporary observers as if it were quite possible that most of western Europe could fall under Turkish rule just as had much of eastern Europe and the Balkans. It was not until the 18th century that the Ottoman Empire began to falter, and even during the 19th century the much discussed "sick man of Europe" was probably far less ill than many supposed. The Turkish performance in World War I, as survivors of the Gallipoli campaign will confirm, was certainly impressive. There were in Ottoman Turkey elements of very solid foundations upon which the creators of modern Turkey could build with such spectacular results.

Since so much of the history of the Islamic world from the time of the original Arab conquests up to at least the 16th century AD has been dominated by the process of nomad invasion and subsequent empire formation, it is not surprising that Islamic historians have shown considerable interest in the precise workings of this phenomenon. In the 14th and early 15th centuries the question was considered by the Persian historian Rashid al-Din (himself an important adviser to one of the rulers of the Il-Khan Dynasty in Iran, an offshoot of the Mongol Empire founded by Genghis Khan) and by the North African scholar Ibn Khaldun (who had the terrifying experience of actually meeting Timur face to face). Scholars such as these were inclined to detect within nomad empires, even at their very apogee of glory, symptoms of inevitable decay and collapse. They felt that these polities had a strictly limited life, after which they would be replaced by something else even if that was but another nomad empire with very similar origins. This theme has fascinated historians ever since.

Distant view of the Hakkari Mountains in Eastern Turkey.

The relative ease with which nomad empires, such as those created by various Turkish, Mongol and Tungusic groups over the millennia, arose, was very much a consequence of the military advantage which, until the development of firearms, the nomad horseman enjoyed over the defenders of urbanised states. He was extremely mobile, very skilled in the use of weapons and, when battle was joined, ferocious and often highly disciplined. The urbanised world, as the Chinese showed with the Great Wall - and as one can see clearly enough in Turkey today where late Roman and Byzantine fortifications, such as the formidable Theodosian walls of Constantinople, can still be found - could not rely on technology to exclude the nomad for ever. Sooner or later either the defenders' vigilance would weaken or the nomad leaders would hit upon methods to penetrate the most elaborate fortifications, including the exploitation of the defenders' own technology (as the Ottoman Sultan Mehmet II made use of gunpowder and artillery, assisted by the Hungarian expert Urban, in the siege of Constantinople in 1453).

Once established, however, the nomad empire immediately began to face problems arising to a great extent from its very nature. Its hold over the people it had conquered, both city dwellers and settled agriculturalists, called for a ready supply of nomad recruits for the military; but these were not to be found so easily in the conquered territories. Nomad recruitment, in other words, depended in the final analysis upon access to the nomad homelands of the steppes. Here, however, it was always possible that fresh nomad-based polities were arising who would not only inhibit recruiting but also turn in due course into the next stage of nomad invasion and empire formation.

The moment he was deprived of direct contact with the native homeland, the nomad conqueror, be he Turk, Mongol or Tungu, faced a cultural crisis which was usually resolved by adopting significant parts of the civilization of the region conquered, and, in particular, its religion. The Seljuk Turks, who were to play a major part in the establishment of Turkish power in Turkey, provide an excellent example of such a process.

Seljuk was the semi-legendary leader of a clan within a Turkish group generally known as the Ghuzz or Oghuz whose ancestral home appears to have been somewhere north of Lake Balkhash (today in Soviet Siberia). The Ghuzz were, in fact, little more than a loose confederation of sub-tribes or clans who, as often as not, were at war with each other, but who still possessed a sense of identity which was sufficient to make them see themselves as different from other Turks. In the latter part of the 10th century the Ghuzz came under pressure from other Central Asian peoples, including the Kipchak Turks (known later to the Russians as the Polovtsy and to the Byzantines as the Cumans), and the various clans were forced to move westwards. Seljuk and his followers split away from the rest of the Ghuzz and migrated to the region of the Jaxartes River (Syr Darya) where, after a possible brief flirtation with Nestorian Christianity, the Seljuk clan finally abandoned its traditional shamanism (characteristic of so many Turko-Mongol groups) for Islam, which it embraced with extreme fervour.

It was as fresh converts to Islam (Sunni) that the Seljuks by a process of dramatic and sudden events so typical of nomad history suddenly found themselves masters of Iran. From here to the conquest of the Levantine coast and Anatolia was but a logical step forward. The key date for the historian of Turkey is 1071 when the Seljuk leader Alp

Arslan defeated and took prisoner the Byzantine Emperor Romanes Diogenes at the battle of Manzikert (Malazgirt, some 50 kms north of Ahlat and Lake Van in eastern Turkey), which confirmed Seljuk domination over the greater part of Anatolia. In less than a century the Seljuks had evolved from shamanist Turkish tribesmen in remote Central Asia to devoutly Sunni Islamic and culturally (at least at Court level) Persianised defenders of the eastern Mediterranean; this included the holy city of Jerusalem, against not only the Byzantines and the Crusading knights of Western Christendom, but also the Fatimid Caliphs of Cairo whose sphere of influence prior to the Seljuks had extended northward through Palestine and Syria to the Byzantine border in Anatolia.

The Seljuk Empire was subjected to the classic strains already referred to. It depended for its military reinforcement upon the recruitment of fresh bodies of Turks, many of whom did not share the Seljuk historic roots. On its eastern frontier, where it was in touch with the nomad steppe lands of Central Asia, it was confronted by other nomadic states both Turkic and non-Turkic. By the end of the 12th century the Seljuk empire had failed to survive these external pressures: from one of the great powers of Asia it had shrunk to highly unstable dominion over those Anatolian tracts which it had conquered from the Byzantines. This was to cut the Seljuks off from the Central Asian recruiting grounds and make them dependent upon their own resources for their survival against both external and internal military and cultural threats. Out of this situation (but not, it was to transpire, under Seljuk leadership) was to emerge one of the major Turkish components of the Turkey we know today.

The final stage of Seljuk isolation from access to Central Asia came in the 13th century with the arrival in Iran and the Levant of a branch of the Genghiskhanid Mongols, the Il-Khans, a dynasty founded by one of Genghis Khan's grandsons, Hulagu (younger brother of Kubilai, ruler of China and founder of the Yuan Dynasty). In the middle of the 13th century the arrival of Hulagu's horde had a devastating effect upon the balance of power in Syria and Palestine, then a field in which Seljuks, Crusaders, and the Mamluks of Egypt (who had just overthrown the Ayyubids) were contending with each other. After overwhelming Iran, which was to become the Il-Khan centre for the next century, Hulagu's armies went on in 1258 to destroy Baghdad and put an end to the Abbasid Caliphate. They then took over much of what is today Syria and penetrated deep into Anatolia. The Seljuk capital Konya was sacked by the Mongols who became the de facto overlords of the Seljuk Sultanate of Rum until, in the early 14th century, they effectively annexed the bulk of its territories.

The Seljuk Sultanate of Rum had from the outset had to confront the fact that there were in Anatolia many Turkish groups who were not Seljuk. Some had already been established there, like the Danishmendids, before the Seljuk arrival; and new Turkish parties continued to turn up throughout the Seljuk era. By the time the Il-Khan Mongols appeared on the scene the Seljuk Sultanate had in fact

Seljuk türbe near Lake Van, Mt. Süphan behind.

disintegrated into a collection of beyliks, or minor emirates. Some were under petty Seljuk princes and some under Turkish chieftains with no dynastic connection to the Seljuks whatsoever; all were struggling to cope with the problems presented by the migration into Anatolia of yet more small Turkish nomadic groups (often the word Turkoman is used for such as these), many of which had started out from Central Asia and Iran as refugees from Mongol devastation, but who soon threatened such political stability as remained in Anatolia.

The Seljuk sultanate, despite its nomadic origins, was very much a state based on towns as well as pastoral steppes. Konya, the capital, was considered by the German Crusaders (who attacked it in 1190) to occupy about the same area as Cologne, then one of the very few cities of any size north of the Alps. While Konya still has some of the finest architectural monuments of the Seljuk period, it has lost its walls and outer fortifications. Diyarbakır probably today gives one a better impression of what a walled Seljuk city must have been like. These cities, with their mosques, palaces, public baths, bazaars, caravanserai and citadels, were linked by a system of roads which, while certainly based in large measure on the Byzantine, Roman and Persian network dating back many centuries, was modified to converge on the new capital, Konya (which had been the old Roman fortress town of Iconium). Along the major routes were constructed fortified caravanserai, or hans, the remains of which must today be numbered among the most impressive of Seljuk monuments.

To the traveller acquainted with European medieval architecture there is a great deal that is familiar in the buildings of the Seljuks in Anatolia. The pointed arches of the hans strongly recall the similarly shaped arches of Early English churches which were replacing the rounded arches of the Norman style at just about this time - the parallel here is probably a coincidence. It is no coincidence, however, that Seljuk fortifications are very similar to those found in the great European castles which were just beginning to spring up in the 12th and early 13th centuries (like King Richard I of England's Chateau Gaillard overlooking the Seine in northern France). The connection here lies in the Crusades which enabled many ideas from the eastern Mediterranean to make their way into western Europe. A most intriguing

illustration of this process can be seen in the round churches of the Knights Templar (there is an excellent English specimen in Cambridge) which are clearly modelled upon the Seljuk türbe or kumbet, the funerary structure with its circular or polygonal central tower capped with a pointed roof, of which there are so many examples still surviving in Anatolia.

The Seljuk monuments of Konya, Kayseri, Erzurum and the other great cities of Anatolia which date back to this period, demonstrate another feature of the Seljuk world. Seljuk art and architecture, while easy enough to identify as Seljuk, yet in many respects are but a branch of a Turko-Iranian style which is to be found in a broad belt extending eastwards across Asia from Anatolia through Iran into Central Asia, Afghanistan and Northern India. There are numerous parallels between the Seljuk buildings of Anatolia, for example, and the earliest Turkish monuments of the Indian capital, Delhi, those erected by Qutb-ud-din and his immediate successors in the late 12th and early 13th centuries.

The Seljuks in Anatolia, in other words, possessed at least at Court level a culture which was Central Asian and Iranian in its origins, rather than Anatolian. It was a culture, however, which was certainly influenced by peculiarly Anatolian elements including the civilisation of Byzantium. This was almost surely so in the administration of the territory which the Seljuks had conquered, where old methods, even if modified to suit Islamic legal concepts, persisted. What also must have persisted to a great degree was the original population.

It is easy to get the impression that somehow after Alp Arslan had defeated Romanes Diogenes in 1071 a vast extent of what had been part of the Byzantine Empire became Turkish in every possible way; and, moreover, that the Turkish population so suggested by this process was nothing but Seljuk. In practice, of course, things worked out quite differently. Anatolia had been penetrated by conquerors from time to time throughout recorded history. In general the invaders established themselves as a ruling class controlling a population that in the main consisted of a mixture of peoples who had always been in Anatolia, peoples who had gradually migrated there rather than arrived as conquerors, and the remains of the now overthrown previous conquering classes. There were periods, such as the 7th and 8th centuries AD for example, when waves of invasion and almost continual war severely reduced the Anatolian population; but there were always some survivors, quite sufficient to carry on old traditions. This highly mixed population, moreover, divided itself between the city dwellers on the one hand and the rural inhabitants on the other. The former could be representative of peoples who had been settled for millennia and were fully aware of the complexities of urban civilisation: the latter could well be nomadic in their way of life, and still retaining traditions which had their roots in regions a long way removed from Anatolia.

Nomads had been coming into Anatolia from the earliest times, some to reinforce the urban populations and some to continue their traditional economy on the Anatolian plains. Such nomads were absorbed easily enough into this rural environment essentially akin to that of the Central Asian steppes, when, as began to happen at least in early Byzantine times, they shared a similar Central Asian background. One group of Huns, for example, could easily merge with another. The Roman historian Ammianus Marcellinus implies this phenomenon when he discusses the strange mixture of peoples, some Germanic and some Turkic, who piled up on the Roman frontier in Thrace just before it collapsed at the battle of Adrianople (Edirne) in 378 AD. Some of the tribes who broke through into Roman territory on that fateful occasion have, or at least their ruling clans have, a well established place in the historical record. Others are certainly unrecorded; and some of them might well have decided to go eastwards rather than westwards from Thrace and have found the crossing of the straits between Europe and Asia no insuperable barrier to their passage to Anatolia. We know, moreover, that peoples of nomadic origin, Teutonic, Slav and Turkic, were recruited into the East Roman and Byzantine armies; and many of these, their service time expired, were settled in Anatolia to add to the ethnic complexity of the population.

What is certain is that from early Byzantine times onwards Anatolia was a reservoir of manpower without which the Byzantine armies could not be reinforced and the Byzantine defences manned. It was, in other words, to the Byzantines what the Central Asian steppes were to the classic Turko-Mongol-Tungusic nomad-based empires. The loss of most of Anatolia meant the eventual collapse of Byzantine military strength: the rest of the Empire was no substitute for this fertile breeding ground of fighting men able by virtue of their background to cope with the ferocity of newly migrating nomads.

Anatolia, what used to be called Asia Minor or Turkey in Asia, possesses certain geographical features which have dominated its history for as long as any evidence exists. This huge peninsula jutting out from the western edge of the Asian landmass is in one respect part of the eastern Mediterranean coastline: in another respect, however, it is a westwards extension of the high plateaux and mountain ranges which stretch eastwards across Iran to Afghanistan and the frontiers of the Indian subcontinent. In its coastal aspect, the Asia Minor peninsula falls very much into the historical context of the eastern Mediterranean which was dominated by Greece, Rome and Byzantium. Its mountainous interior, on the other hand, belongs more to the mainstream of Asian history which was so greatly affected by the movements of nomads and the rise and fall of their imperial structures.

The concept of a clear cut division between the coastal plain and the mountainous interior is far too simplistic to serve as a model of particular value in the analysis of the pattern of Turkish history. Within Anatolia are a fairly large number of distinct zones defined by natural features which have often sufficed to isolate them from each other. Coastal city states could coexist with interior nomad empires. The hinterland could be divided between several polities with

differing cultures, religions and systems of government. The eastern part of Anatolia, where the peninsula stretches towards northern Iran and the Caspian Sea like some kind of giant root penetrating into the body of the western Asian mainland, gives access to at least three regions of enormous historical importance; to the Caucasus between the Black and Caspian Seas, to northern Iran, and to the upper reaches of the great Tigris and Euphrates Rivers which flow into the Persian Gulf. South central Anatolia, where the peninsula joins the mainland, not only touches the extreme northeastern corner of the Mediterranean in the Gulf of Iskenderun, but also provides a gateway to the deserts of Syria which lead eastwards to Mesopotamia and southward to the Red Sea and Egypt. Since all these areas of contact have been among or close to the cradles of civilization, it is not surprising that by one or other of them a diversity of influences both cultural and political have found their way into Anatolia over the millennia.

The western portion of Anatolia leads on to quite another world. Across the Bosphorus and the Dardanelles lies the road to Thrace, where there is, as it were, a triple junction. To the west is the way, either through the Balkans or by sea, to Italy and the western Mediterranean. To continue northwards through the Balkans is to reach the heart of Central Europe, today perhaps symbolised by cities like Budapest, Vienna and Bratislava. To bear northeast around the Black Sea is to embark upon one of those routes into the steppe country which, if followed to its conclusion, will lead one to the frontiers of the Chinese Empire.

Turkey in Europe, Turkish Thrace, by virtue of this geographical connection with Central Asia via what is today Russia, was just as much involved with the phenomena of nomad society and politics as was that part of Anatolia in contact with Iran, Mesopotamia and Syria. Before the Turko-Mongol-Tungusic nomads began to appear on the frontiers of western Asia and Europe, perhaps somewhere around the 4th century AD, the great plains of what is now the Soviet Ukraine and their extension across the lower Danube to Thrace were as active in nomad migration, conflict and state building as was ever to be the case in the steppe land of Central Asia.

Nearly all these early nomads were linguistically Indo-Europeans. Indeed, the bulk of the speakers of Indo-European languages in Europe (which means, in fact, the majority of the present European population, Latin, Slav, Teuton, Scandinavian and Celt) have their roots in nomad migrations going back to these times, migrations in their essentials not very different from the later, and better documented, movements of the Seljuk Turks from further Central Asia to the shores of the Mediterranean. The origins of the Indo-European phenomenon are still not understood. What is certain is that somewhere about 2000 BC peoples of this language group were turning up on the borders of the Indian subcontinent, the so-called Fertile Crescent and the eastern frontiers of Europe; and the process went on for well over two thousand years.

When earlier nomads, such as were all the Greek tribes who eventually settled in the Greek peninsula, the Aegean islands and the southwest coast of Anatolia, had developed sophisticated urban civilizations, newer nomads continued to arrive, often to be despised by their predecessors. The Macedonians, for example, were members of the Greek world who entered on the scene of written history while still more or less nomadic. Other Greeks thought that they were barbarians, that their speech sounded rather like the bleating of sheep. Yet they were really only Greek nomads in a slightly earlier stage of evolution; and they went on to show that Greek nomadism was in its way a force to be compared to that of Turk or Mongol in later centuries.

The first of the ancient Empires based on Anatolia of which we have any literary knowledge (Troy always excepted) is that of the Hittites, a people mentioned in the Old Testament but only demonstrated to have actually existed by scholars in the last quarter of the 19th century. The Hittites were initially detected in northern Syria in the 1870s when inspired guess work attributed to them some inscribed stone fragments. It was not until the very end of that century that the ruins at Boğazköy, right in the heart of Anatolia, were connected with the Hittites. Excavation was to begin in 1906. It soon became clear that at Boğazköy was the heavily fortified city of Hattusas, capital of a Hittite empire which, at its greatest, controlled much of eastern Anatolia as well as the Syrian lowlands extending southwards almost to Damascus.

The Hittite origins are obscure. Some time around 2000 BC a nomadic group of speakers of an Indo-European language must have migrated into Anatolia, perhaps from northern Iran, and established themselves as the ruling clans of what by c.1750 BC was developing into an impressive empire, to some extent at Hurrian expense. The Hurrians, with their heartland in the region of Lake Van, were in origin neither Semitic nor Indo-European, though eventually they acquired cultural features derived from both, the Indo-European element coming from the kingdom of Mitanni to their east. Both the Hurrians and Mitanni, while they occupied territory which is today part of the Republic of Turkey, belong more to the history of Mesopotamia than to that of Anatolia; but they do seem to have provided a barrier of sorts against the eastward expansion towards Iran of the Hittites, and for a while the Mitanni seriously challenged Hittite power in Syria and Mesopotamia.

At its height, during the period between c.1400 and

Paved road at the Hittite capital of Boğazköy.

c.1200 BC, the Hittites defeated the mighty Egyptian Empire in a contest for control over the northern part of Syria. The text of an Egyptian-Hittite treaty dating to about 1270 BC and relating to this conflict exists in clay tablets discovered both at Boğazköy and in Egypt. Shortly after this event, the Hittites, like so many other empires and states in the ancient Levant, had to face during the 12th century BC what is often referred to as the migration of the "Sea" or "Island" people, an event described with considerable alarm in Egyptian inscriptions. The precise nature of the movement of these people, and exactly who they were, is uncertain; but there is little doubt as to the main consequences of their arrival. Perhaps what we have here is some cataclysmic disturbance of populations in the Eurasian landmass which, among its other effects, produced fresh post-Mycenaean Greek migrations into the Aegean littoral. In Anatolia it seems to have resulted in the abandonment of Hattusas; but some kind of Hittite presence persisted in southeastern Anatolia and in Syria, in territory which lay adjacent to the great Assyrian Empire, up to about 700 BC. The Taurus Mountains provided a number of particularly suitable remote strongholds where Hittite rule could survive.

The material remains of the Hittites show a state which was prepared to borrow many cultural elements from its neighbours, often in rather unexpected ways. Thus the Hittite Empire, so its surviving literary records, such as clay tablets, seals and stone inscriptions, indicate, made use of some eight distinct languages. Royal documents employed two, Hittite (which was Indo-European) and Akkadian (which was a Semitic language of the Mesopotamian family of languages); but for other purposes, mainly connected with religious ceremonies, languages such as Luwian, Palaic, Hurrian and Sumerian were also employed. Hittite records from Anatolia are nearly all written on clay tablets in that wedge-shaped cuneiform script so characteristic of the civilizations of Mesopotamia. Another writing system, involving strange hieroglyphics, was also used. It became the main Hittite script after the collapse of the Hattusas Empire; and most Hittite hieroglyphic texts, usually stone inscriptions, date from the last phases of Hittite culture.

Both Hittite writing systems, and the languages that they convey, can now be read to a more or less satisfactory extent; and they provide a sufficiently abundant literature to tell us a great deal about Hittite government and religion. They supplement the information provided by the physical remains such as the excavated ruins of Boğazköy and the great galleries of rock carvings at Yazilikaya. The picture which they convey, when all these sources are considered together, is at first somewhat contradictory. In the material remains of the Hittite world there is a great deal that is not Hittite but borrowed from somewhere else, usually from the great civilizations of Mesopotamia to the southeast. There is much that is Mesopotamian in Hittite religion, in system of government, in art and architecture, resulting in a fusion of Semitic and Indo-European traditions. Some deities, for example, can be identified easily enough with the Indo-European pantheon which is also represented in the ancient religions of India and the Greek and Roman worlds; but other Hittite cults of which there is evidence are clearly of Semitic Mesopotamian origin. Reflection, however, can only lead to the conclusion that this is very much what one would expect from a polity with the kind of nomadic origin which has been suggested. The Hittites borrowed, but they also adopted, adapted, and added to their original traditions; just, indeed, as did the Seljuks many centuries later during the course of their physical migration from Central Asia to the Levant, and their cultural migration from nomadic shamanism to Islam and Persianised urbanisation.

The Hittites made way for others, Urartians, Phrygians, Lycians and Lydians, as rulers of the Anatolian interior. The origins of the Urartians are uncertain. They may have migrated into eastern Anatolia from Iran, or (and the two possibilities do not entirely exclude each other) they may have had their roots to a greater or lesser extent in the state of the Hurrians. Like the Hurrians, the Urartians developed their polity from a centre in the region of Lake Van and Mount Ararat. For a period in the 8th century BC their empire extended not only over much of eastern Anatolia but also the northern plains of Mesopotamia. The Urartians, like the Hittites before them, borrowed a great deal of their culture from Mesopotamia; but, particularly in the field of architecture, they took a number of essentially Assyrian forms and added to them something very much of their own. There are archaeologists who see in the Urartian architectural remains of eastern Anatolia a significant transitional influence between Assyria and the great monuments of Achaemenian Iran like the palace complex at Persepolis. The present town of Van is the site of what was for a while the Urartian capital, Tushpa, and the cliff on which is built the citadel contains Urartian rock-cut tombs and some important Urartian inscriptions; and not far to the north-east of Van is the fortified hill at Toprakkale which was once the Urartian settlement of Rusahina. Like Hurrian, the Urartian language seems to have been neither Semitic nor Indo-European in origin, though it was written in the cuneiform script so characteristic of ancient Mesopotamia.

The Phrygians, at about the same time, established themselves as successors to the Hittites in that part of Anatolia in which the city of Hattusas (Boğazköy) had once flourished. Unlike the Urartians, the Phrygians were Indo-Europeans. Their polity persisted in central Anatolia until it

The Urartu citadel at Van.

was finally suppressed by the Persians in the 6th century BC. Their capital at Gordium, a hundred miles or so to the west of Ankara, has been extensively excavated in recent years to reveal a most impressive citadel. Here, one presumes, the half-legendary king Midas once reigned. The Phrygians constructed numerous rock-cut monuments. The precise nature of their culture is puzzling. The writing system is derived from the Greek and other Greek influences are evident; yet one certainly cannot look on the Phrygians as some remoter outpost of Greek cultural expansion or diffusion. There is a powerful Anatolian component here.

The Lydians and Lycians occupied the southwest corner of Anatolia where their nearest contacts were not with Mesopotamia and the sphere of the old Hittite Empire but with the eastern Mediterranean. The Lydian capital was Sardis. In the 7th century BC, under Gyges, the Lydians began to build an extensive state in western Anatolia both at the expense of the Phrygians and of the Greek coastal states. During his reign western Anatolia came under attack from nomads displaced from the plains along the northern littoral of the Black Sea. These people, the Cimmerians (whose name still survives in Crimea), effectively suppressed for a time the Phrygian kingdom; but Lydia managed not only to survive their incursions, despite Gyges' defeat and death in battle, but to go on, late in its history, to produce the wealthy and, for a while at least, powerful king Croesus so familiar to Greek historians. Many of the Cimmerian invaders were eventually absorbed into the body of the Anatolian population and disappeared. As a state Lydia strongly opposed Greek expansion into the Anatolian interior; and by the end of Croesus' era (546 BC) Lydia had established its dominance over most of the Greek states in western Anatolia, Miletus excepted. The Lydians are usually credited with the invention of coinage. Culturally they were certainly under very great Greek influence; and yet, like the Phrygians, it is legitimate to see in them much that is distinctly Anatolian. All the same, they certainly fall more into the Greek than the Mesopotamian and Iranian side of what was soon to emerge as a major cultural watershed in world history.

The Lycians dominated the extreme western end of the Taurus Mountains to the west of Antalya. Their territory reached the coast; and their culture produced an abundance of rock-cut funerary monuments which were already attracting the attention of European travellers in the late 18th century. These, both cave tombs and free-standing structures, are among the most abundant and impressive remains of ancient non-Greek Anatolia; but they nearly all date to a fairly late period, the 5th century BC or later, by which time the history of Anatolia had been drastically changed by the spread of Greek settlement along the southern coast and the penetration of Persian power into the interior. In political structure Lycia was for much of its history more a federation of towns than a centralised state such as was Lydia or Phrygia. Its most important city was Xanthus, near the modern Kaş.

The rise of the Phrygian, Lydian and Lycian and other lesser Anatolian states coincided with the early phases of active settlement along the western and southern coastal strip of Asia Minor of colonies of people who are clearly recognisable as Greek. No doubt the whole process of replacement of the old powers of Anatolia, the Hittites on the east and whoever it was that built the citadel of Troy VI on the west, by these new polities was part and parcel of that historical movement which gave rise to the Aeolian, Ionian and Dorian Greek states and which is echoed in the Homeric story of the Trojan War.

The Ionian Greeks who dominated the southwestern coast of Anatolia and its adjacent islands possessed a significantly different tribal history, in their nomadic past, from other Greek groups who established themselves in Europe. These differences were further reinforced by contact between the Ionians and the Anatolian states they encountered like the Phrygians, Lycians and Lydians, and from the indigenous Anatolian inhabitants who inevitably were incorporated into any Greek colony however Hellenic the official culture and the ruling aristocracy might claim to be.

There can be little doubt that the basic population of Anatolia did not reflect exactly the rise and fall of empires and kingdoms. From the neolithic, c. 6000 BC or thereabouts as witness the discoveries made at sites such as Çatal Hüyük southeast of Konya, there were settled populations in Anatolia, constantly being reinforced by nomadic migration, which remained where they were whoever might be the ruling class and whatever might be the dominant culture. Most authorities are agreed, in other words, that there had evolved by at least the Hittite period something that we might call an Anatolian people which can be considered to a great measure ancestral to the Anatolians of today. Contact by newcomers with these grass roots inevitably brought about cultural change on both sides, sometimes dramatic and sometimes subtle. The Ionian Greeks were no exception in that they were profoundly influenced by the fact of their presence in Anatolia. Even in Classical times, for example, they possessed quite distinctive architectural concepts, some of which, such as the rams' horn volute on the Ionic capital, probably show influences which were shared with regions much further to the east.

While contact between the Ionian Greek world and that of the Greeks on the European mainland always remained close - the excellent internal sea communications of the Aegean ensured that - it did not tend naturally towards political unity. Before the conquest of Alexander of Macedon there never was anything approaching a single empire which united all the Greek settlements. Indeed, the tendency of the Greeks, in contrast to the major powers of the Anatolian interior, was to create city states of very limited territorial extent rather than to acquire control over large expanses of territory. When Greek empires did emerge, as under the Athenians in the 5th century BC, they possessed more of the features of federation and alliance than of imperial integration; and they were extremely unstable. For a while the Athenians dominated the Anatolian Greek cities and states; but neither did they manage to bring the whole of mainland Greece under their control nor did they endeavour to penetrate any distance into the Asian interior. Spartans, Thebans and others achieved no more and for no greater period of time. What the Greeks excelled at was the establishment of

colonies. These might retain very close political ties with the mother city or, as was perhaps more usual, preserve connections which had with time become little more than those of sentiment. By process of the foundation of new city states the Greek world expanded rapidly around the shores of the eastern Mediterranean, and in the western Mediterranean it was only checked by the encounter with the comparable growth of the Phoenicians. As colonisers in this sense Miletus was outstanding among the Ionian Greek city states. The Milesians by the 6th century AD had ringed the Black Sea with settlements (they are said to have founded some ninety colonies in all). This process, however, neither produced imperial structures in any but the most transitory sense, nor did it bring about any depth of Greek penetration into the hinterland.

The whole pattern of Anatolian history was changed when it became involved in a conflict between Persia and the city states of the eastern Mediterranean. Anatolia has often been described as being a kind of bridge linking Asia to Europe. Up to the point of the Perso-Greek conflict this had not, in fact, been the case. Peoples did not cross over to the heart of Asia from Europe or vice versa by way of the Anatolian peninsula. Rather, peoples from Europe or Asia made their way by various routes into Anatolia only to find their further progress blocked either by the nature of the terrain or the presence of some polity opposed to their further expansion. Thus on the one hand the Hittites never advanced into the western part of Anatolia, where there existed states like Arzawa, whose history is shadowy but whose power was clearly sufficient to restrain the mighty empire ruling Hattusas; while on the other hand no state either based in western Anatolia or entering Anatolia from the European mainland and islands is recorded to have moved through to Iran or Mesopotamia or, even, Syria. Anatolia, in other words, was a buffer rather than a bridge. The situation, however, changed dramatically with the coming of the great Perso-Greek crisis, in which the role of Anatolia was crucial.

About the time that the last petty Hittite states along the Syrian edge of Assyria were coming to an end, c. 800-750 BC, a new power was just beginning to grow on the eastern flank of Mesopotamia. The Medes, essentially a group of nomadic tribes with their centre in the Zagros mountains near the modern Iranian city of Hamadan (Ecbatana), began to coalesce into the nucleus of a new state, which by the beginning of the 7th century BC had managed to free itself from Assyrian domination. Half a century later the Medes were creating an empire which had the strength to occupy the centre of the great Assyrian Empire. They were also able to take over those portions of Anatolia which had been the Hittite (and then Urartian) heartland, and by 585 BC they had established a common frontier with the Lydians along the River Halys (Kizilirmak).

In 550 BC the Medes were conquered by the Achaemenian Persians under Cyrus. The Achaemenian line, with its roots among the tribes occupying Fars, that part of Iran in the region of Shiraz, was in ethnic background very similar to that of the Medes, Indo-European in language and culture; but it was to produce a sequence of leaders with ideas of imperial conquest on a scale which had not hitherto been seen in the Ancient World. Cyrus took his first major step towards this objective when he defeated Croesus, King of Lydia, and crossed the old Median frontier on the Halys into Lydia. Next, almost inevitably, Cyrus' influence was spread from the Anatolian plateau down to the Ionian Greek city states of the southwestern coast, most of which in one way or another were made to acknowledge Persian supremacy. Cyrus then went on to extend his empire eastwards to the banks of the River Oxus and the plains of northwestern India. In 539 BC he invaded Mesopotamia and captured Babylon. A few years later Cyrus' successor Cambyses conquered Egypt, thus bringing effectively all the centres of ancient civilization of the Near East under a single ruler.

The new Persian state was much concerned with the creation of lines of communication to bind its widespread conquests together. For the first time in history serious attention was paid to road construction in Anatolia: the Achaemenians from Cyrus onwards, for example, worked on the building of a military road linking Sardis, the Lydian capital, to Susa, the new Achaemenian capital in Mesopotamia, by way of the Cilician Gates through the Taurus mountains and Nineveh on the Tigris. The Mediterranean was now the western frontier of an imperial structure which stretched right across Asia to the plains of northern India.

The inevitable conflict between Greece and Persia has come down to the western world, through the writings of the Greek historians, as essentially a struggle between freedom and tyranny, between good and evil. The oriental despotism of the Achaemenian state is contrasted with the democratic individuality of the citizens of the Greek city states. From this version of the epic there penetrated into the European consciousness the concept of Asia as being synonymous with barbarous absolutism. Since the main field of this particular conflict was the eastern Mediterranean, the identification of Anatolia with that region where the two value systems and the two cultures met was unavoidable. The Ottoman Turks, when some 2000 years later they followed roughly the same path of conquest into the Greek world as had the Achaemenian Persians, were somehow identified in European minds with those great Persian despots, Darius and Xerxes.

In many respects the conventional picture is, if not totally false, at least greatly distorted. The Achaemenian Persians had, in fact, a closely related origin to the Greeks in the early history of Indo-European migration. The cultural level of the empire which they created was in no way inferior to that of the Greek city states. The monotheism of the Achaemenians probably had as profound an effect upon the subsequent development of western civilization as did anything contributed by the Greek philosophers. Without the enlightened religious policy of Cyrus and Darius, indeed, it is unlikely that the Old Testament would have been edited into the shape that has come down to us today: it was Cyrus, after all, who not only permitted the Jews to return to Palestine from their Babylonian captivity but also encouraged the reconstruction of the temple at Jerusalem, all of which clearly had a most profound effect upon the evolution of Judaic theology. Not all Greeks opposed Persian rule: indeed, a surprising number of them were prepared to enter the service of the Great King. Many Greeks fought with the Persians as mercenaries, and, it seems, a significant number of these decided to settle within the confines of the Persian empire when their service had expired.

For some two centuries the Achaemenian Persians dominated Anatolia and endeavoured with varying degrees of success to control the coastal Ionian Greek settlements. Suprisingly, these years have left very little in the Turkish archaeological record. This period of Turkish history, as has been noted, has conventionally been represented in western historiography as the age when Oriental despotism threatened enlightened Greek polities. From the purely Turkish point of view, perhaps, more significant is the fact that during these years, from Cyrus' defeat of Croesus of Lydia in 546 BC to the defeat of the last of the Achaemenians, Darius III, at Issus by Alexander of Macedon in 334 BC, the whole of what is today the modern state of Turkey (and a great deal besides) was under the rule of a single power. Among the multitude of political achievements of Cyrus the Achaemenian must be included, therefore, the founding of the concept of a united Anatolia.

The Achaemenian presence in Anatolia resulted, at least as far as recorded history is concerned, in another innovation in that it produced the first chronicles of major military campaigns to be launched westwards across the narrow waterway of the Bosphorus and the Dardanelles. Darius had cause to cross over to Europe a number of times. In c.513 BC he invaded Thrace, penetrating beyond the delta of the Danube along the shores of the Black Sea into the lands of the Scythians. On this occasion one of his engineers (a Greek from Samos) constructed a bridge of boats across the Bosphorus. A quarter of a century later Darius had again to consider the problem of the transfer of armies across the Straits. Ionian Greek rebellion, supported by mainland Greek states, necessitated Persian reaction. In 492 BC the Persian general Mardonios transported a powerful force across the Dardanelles by boat as the initial stage in a campaign which was to lead to Persian disaster at Marathon two years later. In 480 BC Darius' successor Xerxes looked once more for a final solution of the Greek problem and launched another massive army across the Dardanelles, this time using a double bridge of boats over which hundreds of thousands of men passed.

Persian invasion was eventually contained by the Greeks of the mainland; but the Anatolian Greek settlements remained under varying degrees of Persian rule or influence, and the existence of the empire of the Great King persisted as a constant factor in Greek international politics. It is probable that it was only the divided nature of Greek city state society, presenting as it did no serious threat to the Persian Empire, that prevented the Great King from again despatching a vast army across the Hellespont (Dardanelles) to teach the Greeks a lesson. By the same token, it was the lack of Greek unity that prevented a Greek commander from planning a campaign in the opposite direction, both to free the Ionian Greek states from Persian dominion and, which was perhaps more important, to eliminate the Persian threat to all of Greece by destroying the Persian strongholds in Anatolia.

The rise of Macedon as the dominant power in Greece, mainly achieved between 346 and 336 BC, created a situation in which the balance of power between Persian Anatolia and the Greek world was bound to be contested. When the energetic and ambitious Alexander at the age of twenty became King of Macedon in 336 BC following the murder of his father Philip, a crisis was inevitable. The resultant conflict between the rising empire of Macedon and the established dominion of the Persian Great King was certainly not an ideological clash between democracy and despotism; Alexander, in his way, had quite as despotic a cast of mind as did Darius III. It was, rather, a struggle between two imperialisms for control over the eastern Mediterranean.

What was surprising about this struggle was its dramatic outcome. Alexander invaded Asia Minor in 334 BC, crossing the Dardanelles and defeating a hastily assembled Persian force on the Asiatic side at Granicus. While Alexander moved through Antatolia, Darius III gathered a great army. In November 333 BC the two armies met on the plain of Issus, not far from Antakya (Antioch). The Persians were decisively defeated and the whole of Anatolia was Alexander's. (It is interesting that in this campaign the Persians were relying as they so often had before on large numbers of Greek mercenaries, many of whom considered the Persians to be less alien that the Macedonians.) In 331 BC, after taking over the whole of the Syrian and Palestinian coast as well as the Persian possessions in Egypt, Alexander crossed the desert into Mesopotamia where he faced what was to prove to be the final stand of Darius III the Great King, at Gaugamela near Nineveh. Darius, decisively defeated, escaped, only to be murdered by one of his commanders.

After Gaugamela the conquest of the eastern part of the old Achaemenian Empire proceeded rapidly. The whole of what is today Iran, plus that Central Asian extension between the Oxus and Jaxartes Rivers, was occupied, and Macedonian armies took over the remoter satrapies in Afghanistan and northwest India. Several cities bearing Alexander's name were founded all over the Achaemenian Empire, some in remote corners of Transoxiana and Afghanistan (Bactria): perhaps part of the population of the new settlements was made up of retired Greek mercenaries formerly in Achaemenian service. By 323, when Alexander died unexpectedly at Babylon just 33 years old, the Macedonian empire had grown into the largest yet known in the Eurasian landmass, including virtually all the ancient centres of civilization of the Fertile Crescent along with northwestern India at the one extreme and mainland Greece at the other. Linking the Greek and the non-Greek parts of this unique edifice was the Anatolian peninsula.

To Alexander the Anatolian peninsula was less important for itself, at least outside the area of the Greek city states, than as the main line of communication between the eastern Mediterranean and the Persian territory in Mesopotamia where lay one of the gateways to the Iranian plateau. To the north of the line of the royal Persian road from Sardis eastwards there were regions, often loosely known as Cappadocia, which were of no immediate interest. These were generally left in the hands of non-Hellenistic rulers, often of Medean, Achaemenian or Parthian (that is to say Iranian) origin. This situation persisted, indeed, right up to the period of Roman conquest in the first century BC; and it would be true to say that throughout Roman times there was something distinctly Anatolian, just as there had been since long before the Hittite age, about the people and the states on the central plateau of Asia Minor. Cappadocia, for example, became formally a Roman province only in the lst century AD.

The Empire of Alexander, as indeed also the Empire of the Achaemenians which it replaced, was in many respects more like a nomad empire than the elaborately structured and administered states created in Egypt and Mesopotamia. The Egyptian and Mesopotamian empires, though they underwent changes of dynasty from time to time, possessed a continuity of both culture and patterns of government which was quite remarkable. Perhaps the only later parallel for them is to be found in Imperial China. To some extent longevity may have emerged from economic necessity. Both in Egypt and Mesopotamia the state was (through state religion and ritual as much as government) required to control elaborate irrigation systems without which the population could not survive. The Nile and the twin rivers of Mesopotamia, the Tigris and the Euphrates, more or less dictated the terms of history. Neither the empire of the Achaemenians nor its Macedonian replacement possessed this economic logic. Both incorporated the old empires of Egypt and Mesopotamia; and, on their collapse, Egypt and Mesopotamia survived as entities in their own right, although under alien dynasties. The greater structure, however, was arbitrary. It depended upon the charisma of the leadership and the continued loyalty of tribal groups, most of them nomadic or deriving from a nomadic tradition (as did, indeed, many of the Greeks), to man the armies which in the last analysis were the glue which held the various portions of the empire together. In maintaining this adhesive the Achaemenians were rather more successful than was Alexander; but by the time of Issus the Achaemenians were in decline.

The logic behind Alexander's creation was even weaker than that which sustained the empire built by Cyrus and his successors. Immediately after Alexander's death the empire was effectively divided up between a number of his generals and advisers. Generally referred to as the Successors (Diadochi) these men were far from united in their policy. Very rapidly the empire broke up into a group of competing states, some of which were soon to pass out of the Greek world entirely. Already in northern Iran, for example, there was arising a new semi-nomad power in the shape of the Parthians who by the beginning of the 2nd century BC were to have taken over much of Iran (from the heirs of Alexander's general Seleucus) and cut off the Greek states in what is today Afghanistan and northwest India from their

The theatre at Miletus.

political and cultural roots in the eastern Mediterranean. By this time, also, the legacy of Alexander was beginning to be absorbed, piece by piece, by another great imperial power of a definitely non-nomadic type, Rome.

The real legacy of Alexander was not so much political as cultural. His imperial creation, and the states that followed it, proved to be an admirable vehicle for both the diffusion and the evolution of the civilization of the Greek city states. The Hellenistic age produced no single Hellenistic empire; but it did give rise to a period of cultural activity which was to continue in the eastern Mediterranean for several centuries. The overwhelming majority of the Greek (and Roman) monuments which make modern Turkey such a fabulous storehouse of Classical Antiquity are the product of this Hellenistic era, though many sites are, of course, much earlier in origin. Didyma, Ephesus, Miletus, Priene, Pergamum and countless other places show the extent to which the city state flourished in the Hellenistic age.

On this Hellenistic base the Romans built when Anatolia passed under their control. Often it is hard to distinguish Roman from Hellenistic; but there was, inevitably, change and evolution. The Romans, for example, introduced their own design of theatre (like the giant one designed by the architect Zeno at Aspendus) and the use of the arch; and they had a concept of scale which their predecessors might have considered a trifle vulgar.

In political terms, however, the Romans returned to what had clearly been the Achaemenian policy at the time of

Cyrus and Darius, and what had been either ignored or beyond the power of Alexander's successors, namely the subjugation of all of Anatolia including the centre and the east. This was a lengthy process which was not completed until the beginning of the 2nd century AD; and never did the remoter parts of Anatolia lose their individual character. The Romans, while they once more brought the whole of what is today Turkey into a single polity, were no more able than their predecessors to impose upon the entire region a cultural uniformity.

The challenger to the Roman domination in the eastern Mediterranean, the Parthian Arsacid Dynasty, owes its origins to tribal groups in Parthia (the tract lying more or less between the modern Iranian centres of Damghan and Mashad) and in Hyrcana (which would be between Teheran and Damghan, controlling the Caspian Gates to the east of Rayy). Arsaces, the founder, died in about 250 BC. By 120 BC his successors, particularly Mithridates I and Phrates II, had expelled the Seleucids, the Hellenistic successors to Alexander the Great, from Iran and Mesopotamia and had penetrated into eastern Anatolia.

The Arsacid Parthian empire would doubtless have continued to expand westwards at the expense of the Hellenistic world, reversing the conquests of Alexander more or less in their entirety, had it not had to face that problem of external security so characteristic of Iranian history over the millennia. No sooner were the Parthians established in Iran than they found themselves under attack from nomads of Central Asian origin.

Such eastern pressures distracted the Parthians at the very moment that Rome was moving in not only to the coastal Hellenistic city states of Asia Minor but also was endeavouring to establish some kind of control over the non-Greek states of the Anatolian interior, such as the Kingdom of Pontus (effectively the hinterland behind the Black Sea coast between Sinop and Trabzon). The inevitable clash between Rome and Parthia was accordingly delayed until the middle of the 1st century BC. When it did come, however, the results were dramatic. In 53 BC a Roman army under Crassus was annihilated by the Parthians at Carrhae (Harran, just inside modern Turkey on the Syrian border). The Parthians thereby set a barrier to Roman expansion southeastwards from Anatolia towards Mesopotamia which was subsequently to be challenged but never to be overcome except on a very temporary basis. The army of the Emperor Diocletian, for example, after a brief period of Roman occupation of Mesopotamia including the capital, Ctesiphon, was to suffer defeat at Iranian hands, under Sassanian rather than Parthian leadership, at the same site of Carrhae in 295 AD.

For the next five centuries or so the frontier of the Roman Empire in the east tended to follow a line which ran southwestwards across Anatolia from a point on the Black Sea coast in the region of the modern Russian town of Batumi to the modern Syrian border south of Urfa, whence it ran more or less due south to the Red Sea at what today is the Gulf of Aqaba. Beyond this line lay routes leading to northern Iran through eastern Anatolia and to the rich cities of Mesopotamia by way of the caravan trails across the Syrian desert which gave rise to such trading settlements as Palmyra (an oasis city in the middle of the desert) and Dura-Europus on the upper Euphrates. Roman attempts to control these routes, and the caravan cities along them, never produced a lasting expansion of Roman dominion. For much of Roman imperial history, therefore, the Roman eastern frontier system ran through eastern Anatolia. Its main function was to protect the central and western parts of Anatolia, and the world of the eastern Mediterranean coast that sheltered behind the Anatolian hinterland, from the threat of invasion from the east by forces which to a greater or lesser degree had a nomadic element in their composition. The arrival of the Seljuk Turks in the 11th century was in essence an event very similar to crises which the Romans had been facing a thousand years earlier.

The Parthian Arsacids were one of the longest-lived dynasties in Iranian history, yet they have left surprisingly little in the way of material remains; and many of their rulers are only known from their numismatic portraits. Perhaps the most dramatic traces of Parthian influence (even if cultural rather than political) in Anatolia are to be found at Nemrut Dag, among the mountains of the modern Malatya district, where the Hellenistic ruler of Commagene, Antiochus I (69-34 BC), constructed a massive funerary hill adorned with colossal sculptures. The frost-crazed stone exhibits a strange mixture of Hellenistic and Iranian influences, some of the latter demonstrating in their turn features that can be traced back to pre-Achaemenian Mesopotamia, which seems to have been characteristic of the art of the Parthians.

The Parthian dynasty persisted in Iran, and in its domination of much of eastern Anatolia, despite occasional Roman thrusts, until the middle of the 3rd century AD, when it was replaced by the Sassanians. The Sassanian founder, Ardashir son of Papak, was a tribal chieftain in Fars, whence had come also the Achaemenians upon whom the Sassanian Kings were so often to model their behaviour and policy. While the arrival of the Sassanians, with strong neo-Achaemenian ideas, profoundly influenced the artistic history of Iran, it did not alter fundamentally the geopolitics of the Iranian-Roman borderland in Anatolia. Rome and Sassanian Iran saw each other as threats; and the long history of their relationship, only terminated by the Arab conquest of Iran in the latter part of the 7th century AD, was one of continual conflict in which the Romans endeavoured from time to time to conquer eastern Syria and extend their frontier to Mesopotamia, while the Iranians sought to extend their rule westwards both in Anatolia and towards the Mediterranean coast in Syria and Palestine.

In this struggle the Iranians scored some notable successes. Shahpur I frustrated the Roman Emperors Gordion III and Philip the Arab in 244 AD after the Romans had penetrated into Sassanian territory almost as far as Ctesiphon (a few miles south of the modern Iraqi capital, Baghdad); and in about 260 AD he prevailed over a fresh Roman attack at yet another major engagement in the region of the old battlefield of Carrhae, taking prisoner the Emperor Valerian whom he subsequently executed. The capture of this particular Roman Emperor is celebrated in a number of vast bas-relief rock carvings in various parts of Iran. A century later Shahpur II overwhelmed a Roman force yet again invading Mesopotamia, this time under the Emperor Julian (known as "The Apostate" because of his attempt to restore the old Roman religion in the place of Christianity) in 363 AD. These campaigns were but a few examples of many which followed very similar patterns, either Roman endeavours to expand across the Syrian desert or down from eastern Anatolia into Mesopotamia where the Sassanians had their effective capital at Ctesiphon, or Iranian efforts to occupy eastern Anatolia and even extend their influence to the Mediterranean seaboard. In the event, Mesopotamia proved just too far for the Romans to hold for any length of time and during the brief periods that they did extend this far eastward their lines of communication were always vulnerable. The Sassanian Iranians, on the other hand, found eastern Anatolia and the Syrian coastal strip likewise a problem. The Roman-Iranian frontier in Anatolia fluctuated in the tract between Lake Van and Kayseri (Caesarea).

There were considerable economic prizes to be won in this conflict. By the time of the Roman occupation of western and central Anatolia and the rise in Iran of the Arsacid Parthians a trade route had emerged which linked China with the eastern Mediterranean, bringing westwards the highly valued silk textiles for the production of which the

Chinese alone knew the secret. This crossed Central Asia from the Chinese inland border, already being marked out by the line of the Great Wall, and reached the West by two paths. One followed a northerly route through what is today Russian territory north of the Caucasus to reach by a number of possible itineraries the shores of the Black Sea; and the other traversed Iran from Transoxiana to Mesopotamia, then continued either through eastern Anatolia or across the Syrian desert to the Mediterranean where it terminated at ports such as those adjacent to what is today the Gulf of Iskenderun.

By Sassanian times the great Eurasian trade route, the Silk Road, had become one of the key elements in the Iranian economy. The demand for eastern goods in general and silk in particular in the Roman world, the greatest single market of antiquity, was insatiable (and the drain on the Roman balance of payments much deplored by contemporary observers). The logic of adding value to the transit dues on this commerce by actually gaining control over one of its western termini in the Mediterranean was inescapable to Sassanian policy makers.

Even when, perhaps by the beginning of the 7th century AD, silk was actually being produced within the Roman world (as a result, so the story has it, of the smuggling out from China of silk-moth eggs), the oriental product was still generally considered to be of better quality and prized accordingly. The cultivation of silk worms, at first in Syria and then in Greece and southwestern Anatolia, did not significantly affect the value of the goods carried both along the overland Silk Road and across the Indian Ocean.

Hunnish invasions of Iran from Central Asia, such as the Hephthalite (White Hun) incursion of 484, may have distracted Sassanian attention for a while from Roman questions; and the Roman world likewise was faced with a sufficiency of problems of its own after the Gothic and other Teutonic nomadic invasions of the 4th century AD had broken much of the Roman frontier system of defence, particularly in Thrace. Nevertheless, Irano-Roman competition continued, with the contest for control over eastern Anatolia a key element.

The climax to the struggle came in the reign of Khusrau (Chosroes) II, 589-628, the last great Sassanian ruler, who took advantage of a crisis in the internal history of the Roman world (or Byzantine, as it had now become) - the overthrow of the Emperor Maurice by the usurper Phocas - to attempt the total destruction of the eastern Roman Empire. The first phase was marked by continual Iranian success, aided by the fact that the Byzantines were facing ferocious attack on the European side from Avar hordes, yet another Central Asian group (perhaps Turkic, perhaps Indo-European) who turned up at this period on the fringes of Europe. In 615 the Iranian army had marched through Anatolia to Chalcedon (Kadiköy), where it was in sight of Constantinople across the Bosphorus. In 619 the Sassanians conquered the Byzantine possessions in Egypt, having previously captured Jerusalem and removed the relics of the True Cross from the Holy Sepulchre. At this stage, they had in effect recreated the Asian part of the Achaemenian Empire much as it had been in the great days of Cyrus and Cambyses.

The Byzantine world was saved by the determined general Heraclius, who had overthrown Phocas in 610, been crowned Emperor and then devoted himself to rebuilding the military strength of the Eastern Empire. By 627 the tide had turned. While the Sassanian Iranians had allied themselves with the Avars in an effort to crack Constantinople in a giant pincer movement, Heraclius had also found his own nomad allies in the shape of the Khazars (possibly another of the Turkic peoples of Central Asia, though the matter is disputed), then the overlords of the lower Volga basin and what was to become the Ukraine. The combined Byzantine-Khazar force drove the Iranians out of Anatolia. In the following year Khusrau was murdered and his son, Kavad II, lost no time in coming to terms with Heraclius. Iranian troops were withdrawn from Egypt, Palestine, Syria and Anatolia; and the pre-war boundaries were restored. It is doubtful, however, if the centres of population in Anatolia completely recovered from the devastation brought about by the Iranian invasion and occupation until modern times.

This particular episode, which marks the end of the struggle between Persia and Rome - Iran was soon to fall to the Arab armies of Islam -, is an admirable demonstration of the most characteristic geopolitical role of Anatolia throughout history, as a kind of barrier or, at least, buffer, between Europe and Asia. The Iranians of Khusrau II were not able to cross over into Europe, nor were their Avar allies able to cross over from Europe to Asia. Constantinople, provided it had an effective command of the sea which enabled it to maintain contact with its allies in the Mediterranean and along the shores of the Black Sea, was ideally situated to act as a door which, when closed, could keep Asia and Europe apart.

This role, to be performed by a fortified base dominating the narrow waterway dividing Thrace from Asia Minor, had been identified in the days of the great struggle between the Greeks and the Achaemenians; and the site of Byzantium was always of strategic importance for this reason. For a while, following the effective Roman occupation of the entire littoral of the Mediterranean basin, it looked as if the central point of the region, the Italian Peninsula, was indeed the geopolitical pivot of the Roman state. By the opening of the Christian Era, however, in the first years of the Empire, it was already becoming apparent that this probably was not the case. The city of Rome might be the administrative centre of the Empire, but in economic terms it was largely parasitic on provinces either in the east or along the North African coast. The two million or so inhabitants of Rome could not be fed without the grain from Egypt and Africa. The city states of the old Hellenistic World were far more energetic in trade and industry than were any of the cities of Italy. Strategically, too, already by the 2nd century AD it was all too clear that Rome was threatened on two major fronts, quite distinct from each other. On the one hand there was the German frontier along the Rhine and the upper Danube. On the other hand there was the double frontier with both Asia and southeastern Europe, with one part in Thrace and the other part in eastern Anatolia and Syria. A single headquarters could not easily command defence against attack from such widely separated sectors.

By the end of the 3rd century AD serious experiments were being made in the administrative division of Rome into more than one region. Diocletian (284-305 AD) actually split the Imperial office into four, though in practice the Emperors tended to operate in pairs. Under Constantine (306-337 AD) the Empire was in theory reunited under one Emperor; but, accepting the geopolitical realities, the capital was shifted from Rome to Byzantium, now renamed Constantinople. By the end of the century the policy of partition was once more revived during the reign of the Emperor Theodosius; and, following his death in 395 AD, partition became permanent with his two sons splitting the Empire between them, Aracadius becoming Eastern Emperor with his capital at Constantinople and Honorius the Western Emperor in Italy. When in 476 AD the Western Roman Emperor Romulus Augustulus was deposed by a Teutonic general, a Herulian called Odovacar, his office lapsed. The Eastern Emperor was now the only Roman Emperor, and Constantinople the only Roman capital.

By 476 AD the dominant problem confronting the rulers of what had been, but no longer was, the Roman Empire in the West was posed by successive waves of Teutonic and other nomad groups who overran western Europe. The Teutonic, or Germanic, threat to Rome had been apparent in the last years of the Roman Republic; but for centuries under the Emperors from Augustus onwards it had been contained along a military frontier outlined by the Rhine and the upper Danube. Following the collapse of the Thracian border in 378 at the battle of Adrianople, the intensity of pressure of these peoples, as well as their numbers and categories, increased at an alarming rate. Quite why this should have been so is still something of a mystery. Did the forced migration of the Hsiung-nu (if they were the ancestors of the Huns) from the Chinese borders centuries earlier precipitate a chain reaction; and was this reinforced by some unrecorded crisis in Scandinavia? Certainly something happened to set the tribes on the move; and it is a fact that behind the Teutonic groups, whose relatives had been around along the Roman frontiers for a long time, there were new peoples of clearly Central Asian origin like the Huns (of Attila fame) and the Avars.

The list of the various Teutonic invaders who penetrated western Europe in the centuries immediately following the crisis at Adrianople in 378 is bewildering. Visigoths, Ostrogoths, Vandals, Alans, Suevi, Gepids, Herulians, Franks, Burgundians, Alemanni, Lombards, Frisians, Saxons, Angles and Jutes, from origins mysterious to varying degrees, these and their kinfolk became the founders of the western European states of the Middle Ages. No sooner had they arrived than they were followed by nomadic peoples of mainly Slav origin (along with a few who may have been Turkic) in a process which many eastern European historians now refer to as "the wandering of the people". Slav groups occupied a broad belt stretching southward from the Baltic to the Adriatic; and it was Slavs of this process of migration, like the Bulgars (originally, it is thought, Turkic but subsequently converted by a complex process of history into Slavs), the Macedonian Slavs, the

Serbs and the Croats, who pressed against the frontiers of East Rome, now Byzantine, just as the Teutons had pressed against West Rome.

For a brief period in the 6th century AD Constantinople reoccupied Rome. Under the Emperor Justinian (527-565 AD) the Byzantines reconquered the Italian Peninsula (where the capital had in the 5th century been moved to Ravenna), as well as parts of Africa and southeastern Spain; but this partial reunification of the old Roman world was shortlived.

By the next century the pattern of the future was clear. The old western Empire, while lacking an Emperor (until Charlemagne's rather artificial revival of the institution in 800 AD), still continued as a cultural entity presided over by the Roman Church; and the Bishop of Rome as Pope acquired many quasi-imperial functions. This western Rome, however, was directed predominantly towards a world where peoples of Teutonic origin formed the new post-Roman ruling classes even if they still did not make up the bulk of the population.

Eastern Rome, had just managed during the crisis of the 7th and 8th centuries AD to survive the attacks of the Avars, the Sassanian Iranians, the Arabs and a host of Slavs. Now it faced in one direction the ruling powers of the western half of the Asian landmass, the dominant Islamic dynasties and various nomadic states, even empires; and in another direction, on the European side, it looked towards a landscape dominated not by Teutons but by Slavs.

This ethnic division between the two portions of the European part of the former Roman Empire quickly acquired theological implications. Just as the Bishop of Rome was the dominant influence in the Teutonic world, so the Patriarch of Constantinople became the key ecclesiastical force in the world where the Slavs had settled, in eastern Europe and, eventually, in Russia.

The Emperor Constantine not only moved the Imperial capital from Rome to Byzantium, henceforth known as Contantinople, but he also effectively turned Christianity into the official religion of the Mediterranean world. This did not mean that the older religions disappeared; and it

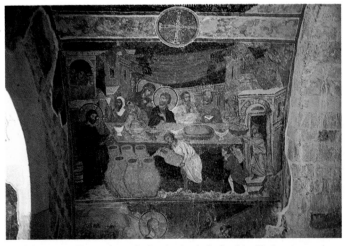

A 13th century Byzantine painting in the Ayia Sophia, Trabzon.

certainly did not mean that the Christian community was united in its theological concepts.

By Constantine's time Christianity had been establishing itself both in the Romano-Greek world and in western Asia for nearly three centuries. Legend, which may indeed represent fact, has it that the Apostle Thomas had brought the faith to India soon after the Crucifixion; and it is highly probable that very early missionaries had spread Christian ideas even further afield than this, into Central Asia and to the borders of the Chinese Empire. One consequence of such wide diffusion was the development of a number of quite distinct schools of Christian thought, the members of any one of which regarded all others as heretics. Right from the earliest times of which we have any record, the growth of Christianity was accompanied by acrimonious doctrinal controversy.

In the spread of Christianity the area that today makes up the Republic of Turkey played a crucial role. From its place of origin in Palestine St. Paul (who came originally from the Turkish city of Tarsus) first took the message of the new faith to the southern Hellenistic cities of Anatolia and the Aegean coast of Greece. By Constantine's time this region of Anatolia probably contained the greatest concentration of Christians and Christian churches in the Roman world; and Christian pockets had been established in the hinterland, in the Urfa (Edessa) region, in Cappadocia, along the Black Sea around Sinop, and in Constantinople and along the shores of the Sea of Marmara. It was also a centre of intense theological speculation in the philosophical tradition of Hellenism. Inevitably the multiplicity of pre-Christian or non-Christian cults which flourished in such cities as Ephesus, and which attracted worshippers from all over the Mediterranean world and beyond, exerted an influence upon the evolution of Christian dogma. Two of the most important ideological gatherings in western history, at Nicaea (Iznik) in 325 and at Chalcedon (Kadiköy) in 451, took place in Asia Minor to endeavour to sort out major doctrinal problems which were constantly appearing.

The identification of Christianity with the Roman state, firmly established (after a brief but abortive attempt by the Emperor Julian in the 360s to restore ancient ways) by the end of the 4th century, meant that in Imperial eyes an orthodoxy of doctrine was inevitably associated with loyalty to the regime; and unorthodox or heterodox views were all too easily equated with treason. Thus the Emperor found himself inextricably involved in the process of supervising the doctrinal purity of the Church. In the Council of Nicaea (325 AD) Constantine sought to neutralise the harmful speculations of an Alexandrian priest, Arius, concerning the nature of the Trinity. The outcome was not entirely successful. The Arian heresy persisted for over a century and infected some of the Teutonic peoples who in the 5th century AD established dominance over the old Roman Empire in the west. There are many traces of Arianism, particularly in relation to baptismal rites, in the exquisite churches of this period which can still be seen in Ravenna.

The Council of Chalcedon in 451 AD was involved in a dispute which left, perhaps, a more permanent mark on the subsequent shape of Christianity. The original argument was between two autocratic clerics, Cyril of Alexandria and Nestorius of Constantinople. The theology, concerned with the nature of the divinity of Christ, need not detain us here. While in themselves the arguments might be seen as no more than squabbles between clerics with too much time on their hands, in practice the outcome of such debates was of the greatest significance. The monophysite view took root in the Coptic-speaking churches of Egypt and the Syrian-speaking churches of Palestine and Syria. To the east, however, among the Christian communities which had settled down under Persian rule in Mesopotamia, the ideas of Nestorius were adopted. As it was from these Mesopotamian churches that Christianity, at least until the 14th century AD, tended to find its way even further eastwards (by c. 640 there was a Christian church at Sian, the capital of the Chinese T'ang Dynasty), Nestorianism became the dominant variety of Christianity in Asia away from the Mediterranean. When, in the latter part of the 13th century, the Mongol ruler of China, Kubilai Khan, wished to open diplomatic relations with the Christian rulers of Europe, he made use of Nestorian clergy to whom he had easy access.

The adoption of Christianity as the official religion of the Roman Empire meant that Emperors encouraged the building of churches as they had previously of temples. The turbulent period between Constantine and the end of the Empire in the West was not particularly propitious for the creation of monuments, though some of the architectural gems of Ravenna date from this time. When Justinian in the 6th century for a moment seemed to be on the way to re-establishing a united Roman Empire, it was inevitable that he should turn his attention to a variety of public works including the construction of churches. The most dramatic result is without doubt Haghia Sophia in Constantinople, the masterpiece of Justinian's two great architects, Anthemius of Tralles and Isidore of Miletus.

Haghia Sophia is not only one of the largest buildings of the ancient world, with a dome over 30 metres in diameter, but it also illustrates a number of basic features of the history of Turkey. There can be no doubt that, as the supreme monument of the Byzantine past, it inspired the Ottoman successors to Byzantium to endeavour to surpass the achievement of Anthemius and Isidore; and in the work of the 16th century architect Sinan many would argue that they succeeded beyond all expectation. Just as Sinan's great buildings in Istanbul, like the Süleimaniye, were in a very real measure the Ottoman answer to the Byzantine Haghia Sophia, so also was Haghia Sophia an answer by that most imperial of all Byzantines, Justinian, to the pretensions of the Great King, the ruler of Sassanian Iran and Byzantium's greatest enemy in the east.

The dome, such a central feature of Byzantine as opposed to Roman architecture (and clearly redolent with symbolism concerning heaven and the world of the spirit), is considered by some scholars to have entered the Roman world by way of Iran. At any rate, there is good evidence that the Iranians discovered the trick of mounting a circular dome upon a square base some time before this problem had been solved in the Roman Empire. The Sassanian Kings erected enormous domed structures, of which some very extensive remains can still be seen at Firuzabad and of which the foundations were excavated at Bishapur, both major Sassanian sites in Fars. The massive dome which Anthemius and Isidore devised for Justinian in Haghia Sophia, therefore, could well symbolise the ability of the Eastern Roman Empire to withstand anything that the Sassanian Great King might choose to hurl against its defences.

Haghia Sophia was, in fact, to be the largest church ever built in the Byzantine Empire, and comparable in scale with the greatest of the western European cathedrals. The Orthodox Christian world was to see nothing like it until the middle of the 16th century when Ivan IV ("the Terrible") built the Cathedral Church of St. Basil in Moscow; and St. Basil, if one cut off the spires and onion domes, would fit inside Haghia Sophia and leave considerable room to spare. In general the churches of Eastern Christianity were surprisingly small, far smaller than the first western European imitations to which they gave rise like St. Mark's Cathedral in Venice.

Of Byzantine small ecclesiastical buildings there are no more fascinating examples than those still to be seen today cut into the lunar landscape of tufa pinnacles in the neighbourhood of Göreme in Cappadocia. They are the remains of hermitages and monastic communities which may have started to grow up as early as the 4th century AD under the inspiration of St. Basil, Bishop of Caesarea, and which continued on well into Seljuk times after the 11th century. The tufa is a particularly soft material and easy to work; but this fact does not alone explain the technical form of the Cappadocian rock-cut churches. There are similar formations in western Europe, in the Puy de Dôme region of France, for instance, which have not given rise to anything like Göreme. One explanation must surely lie in the example in rock-cut architecture already set by the Lycians and others in Anatolia. Here is perhaps another glimpse of that fascinating phenomenon of continuity in Anatolian culture and population despite apparently cataclysmic changes at the Imperial or Royal level. However the chronology of the rock-cut churches of Cappadocia is still a subject of scholarly controversy.

The inheritors of the nothern lands once ruled by the Urartu were the Armenians. Their early history is obscure. By the 5th century BC Armenia was well known to contemporary geographers. An ambassador from Armenia appears in the carvings at Persepolis, the palace of Darius the Great. The Romans found a useful buffer state already in place, although the frequent and confused dynastic troubles made its stability uncertain. At times there was more than one Armenian king, and the Byzantines, who regarded the Armenians as renegade and heretic Christians, were uncertain of their loyalty. Many were resettled in Cilicia or Central Anatolia by the 11th century. Their independence ended with the arrival of the Seljuks; and in the 14th century Mongol raids and earthquakes devastated many of their towns. In the 15th century Timur utterly destroyed what remained, for example at Ani, which had been a town with a population of 100,000 to 200,000, and which was emptied. What does remain today of medieval Armenia are a few isolated but splendid churches, especially at Ani and Akhtamar.

Within a few years of the Sassanian failure to take Constantinople a fresh threat to Byzantium arose from the rather unexpected direction of Arabia. The unification of the Arabs under the inspiration of Islam ushered in a new era in world history of which the first effects were soon felt in the eastern Mediterranean. By 642 AD the Arab armies had occupied the former Sassanian territory in Mesopotamia as well as the Byzantine possessions in Syria, Palestine and Egypt including the cities of Damascus, Jerusalem and Alexandria. The Arabs were now poised on the eastern edge of Anatolia, ready to step into that territory so recently ravaged by the Sassanians. Only internal Arab dissension delayed the inevitable onslaught. The conflict between the founders of the Umayyad Caliphate and the followers of the descendants of Ali, the Prophet's son-in-law, distracted Arab attention for a while; but, once victorious, the Umayyads directed all their energies towards the elimination of Byzantium, their major Mediterranean rival. An initial Arab attack against Constantinople failed in 677 after a three year siege. A second attack, of considerably greater intensity, took place in 717-718 when some 80,000 men in Umayyad service were brought by sea once more to lay siege to the Byzantine capital. The city was defended successfully by the Emperor Leo III the Isaurian, whose theology was certainly influenced profoundly by his experiences. A correlation was made between the rise of superstition and the worship of icons on the one hand and the Islamic threat to the Empire on the other.

After 718 the Islamic challenge to Byzantium was removed for the time being from the immediate proximity of the city walls of Constantinople; but the danger to the Empire was still grave. In 726 an Umayyad army invaded Anatolia and reached the walls of Nicaea (Iznik) before being pushed back by the Emperor Leo III and eventually defeated. The Abbasid Caliphate in the 9th century also turned its attention to Byzantium. In 806 Harun al-Rashid marched through Anatolia to the region of Ankara before being bought off by the Byzantines; and in 838 the Caliph al-Mu'tasim made a further incursion. These expeditions, however, were no more than raiding ventures, albeit on a gigantic scale. Neither al-Rashid nor al-Mu'tasim was able to maintain a position so deep within Anatolia. What these ventures did was to add to the desolation of much of Anatolia which had already been brought about by the earlier conflict with the Sassanians.

Despite these Abbasid excursions, by the middle of the 9th century an Arab-Byzantine border had been established in Anatolia. It was somewhat less favourable to the Byzantines than that which had prevailed prior to the great Sassanian attack of the early 7th century AD. Antioch (Antakya) and Edessa (Urfa) were on the Muslim side of a line which ran from somewhere in the region of Tarsus northeastwards between Sivas and Erzincan to the Black Sea coast somewhat to the east of Trabzon.

Under the early Abbasid Caliphate in the late 8th and early 9th centuries the Muslim hold on this line was the most secure; but in later Abbasid times it began to weaken a little to enable the Byzantines to expand along the Black Sea coast and the shores of the Gulf of Iskenderun into Syria as well as into the eastern Anatolian hinterland. By the opening of the 11th century, with the Abbasids clearly in decline and their claim to the Caliphate being challenged by the Fatimids in Egypt, the Eastern Empire was able to conduct a sustained process of territorial recovery. By the time that the Seljuk Turks arrived upon the scene, the Byzantines had effectively established themselves in Anatolia as far east as a point somewhere between Lake Van and Lake Urmia, indeed almost exactly where the present border of the Turkish Republic runs. Then, of course, came the crisis of Manzikert in 1071 when, as we have seen, the Seljuks shattered the Byzantine hold on the greater part of Anatolia.

In 1071 the Byzantine Empire, though in many respects a pale shadow of what it had been in the days of Justinian, was still one of the major centres of economic activity in Christendom. It enjoyed extensive commercial links with the Islamic polities of the eastern Mediterranean, and, through them, with the expanding Asian commerce of the Indian Ocean. It had retained through its contacts with the littoral of the Black Sea access to overland caravan routes to the Far East which brought not only silks but also gold (so that, unlike the rest of Europe, Byzantium had managed after the 7th century to maintain a gold coinage). It maintained close commercial relations with the rising Italian trading cities like Venice, though not always on the friendliest of terms. Finally, through the rivers of the Ukraine, Byzantium was in direct communication with the emerging Scandinavian (Viking) kingdoms of the Baltic, with which it traded and from which it recruited mercenaries (including the famous Imperial Varangian Guard). This commercial prosperity, based in the last analysis upon the strategic position of Byzantium, persisted despite political disasters; and it goes far to explain why the catastrophe of Manzikert was not, in fact, immediately fatal.

The events of 1071, nevertheless, mark a turning point not only in Turkish history but also that of the world. They ushered in the era of the Crusades during which western Europe tried and failed to extend itself on a permanent basis on to the Asiatic shores of the eastern Mediterranean. They brought about the ultimate downfall of the very Byzantine Empire which they were in part intended to defend. For the Byzantines never really recovered from the sack of

A distant view of Mount Ararat in Eastern Turkey.

Constantinople in 1204 not by the Turks but by the Crusaders, with the Venetians very much to the fore (seeking to take over for themselves the commercial potential of Byzantium, in which ambition they faced fierce competition from the Genoese). Finally, the arrival of the Seljuk Turks brought about those conditions which, two centuries later, were going to permit the rise of the Ottoman Turks as the final victors over Byzantium and the creators of one of the greatest empires ever to emerge in the eastern half of the Mediterranean.

By the eve of the battle of Manzikert in 1071 it can be argued that the present shape of the Turkish Republic had already begun to emerge. The Byzantine Empire by 1071 had shrunk to Anatolia, roughly the equivalent of modern Turkey in Asia, plus a portion of the adjacent European mainland across the Bosphorus and Dardanelles. In 1071 the European portion was rather more extensive, including as it did much of Greece and other Balkan tracts, than it is today; but, from a geopolitical point of view, it performed much the same role in guarding the European shore of the narrows and guaranteeing commercial and political access between the Black Sea and the eastern Mediterranean.

Shortly after 1071, with the occupation of the greater part of Anatolia by the Seljuk Turks, Asia Minor acquired a predominantly Turkish ruling class. This was certainly not the first time that Turkish speakers had found their way on to what is today Turkish territory. The Byzantines had been recruiting as soldiers tribesmen of Turkish origin for centuries; and these, who frequently came along with their entire families and flocks, were often settled in Anatolia which, particularly after the Iranian and Arab incursions of the 7th, 8th and 9th centuries, was considerably less populous than it had been at the height of the Romano-Hellenistic era (when it was generally considered to hold the largest population within the Roman Empire). What was particularly significant after 1071 was that Turkish speakers would from now onwards continue to dominate the government of Anatolia in place of those more or less Romano-Hellenised aristocracies that had prevailed since at least the days of Alexander the Great.

By the time in the middle of the 13th century when the power of the Seljuks had been broken in Anatolia by the Mongols, the Seljuk-Byzantine frontier ran in a great arc from the Mediterranean roughly at the modern port of Marmaris northeastwards inland to Eskişehir, and then along the immediate Black Sea hinterlands to somewhere near Rize east of Trabzon (with the exception of that stretch between Sinop and Samsun, where the Seljuk zone actually came down to the coast). There was also a thin Byzantine coastal strip in the region of Tarsus and the Gulf of Iskenderun. This frontier, which had been established fairly rapidly after Manzikert, remained more or less stable for nearly two centuries, despite the impact of the Crusades which had, as one of their objectives, the expulsion of the Seljuks from the Eastern Empire.

Crusaders, of course, did penetrate the Seljuk border from time to time, the most notable occasions, perhaps, being the traversing of Anatolia by the main army of the First Crusade in 1097-98, and the march of Frederick I Barbarossa, the German Emperor, across Seljuk territory in

1190 on his way to the Third Crusade, during which his troops sacked the Seljuk capital at Konya. The adventure ended in Frederick's death by drowning while crossing a river along the Cilician coastal strip, ironically in Byzantine-held territory; and it had no lasting impact upon the position of the Turks in Anatolia. The Seljuks, by the same token, campaigned across to the Byzantine side of this divide; but the Imperial forces were usually able to contain them or force them back to the de facto border.

During the 13th century the situation changed. While the power of the Seljuks as a ruling dynasty was effectively ended by the Mongol Il-Khans, the Seljuks were in any case, in the final analysis, only a ruling clan and by no means the totality of the Turkish population of Anatolia. The Seljuk migration had been followed by the migration of many tribal groups, some large, some small, either seeking a kingdom of their own or service with some other Turkish dynasty. It is known, moreover, that these Turkish migrants, the Seljuks included, found that a significant number of Turkish tribesmen had in unobtrusive ways preceded them on to the Anatolian highlands. Often the term Turkoman, rather than Turk, is used to distinguish these more humble members of the Turkish migration from Central Asia; but, Turk or Turkoman, these people easily adapted on the one hand to the prevailing Turkish dominated political climate and, on the other hand, preserved traditions of a past and an awareness of a present identity of their own. A number of non-Ghuzz Turkoman groups, such as the Danishmendids with their centre on the Sivas region, had already established what amounted to independent states on Byzantine territory before the arrival of the Seljuks; and they continued to be a major factor in Anatolian politics throughout the Seljuk era. It was all too easy, with the evident failure of the Seljuk line, for leaders of such groups to aspire to even greater power. From such a background, of Turks with strong tribal identity but not associated with the Seljuk mainstream, was to emerge the empire which would consolidate Turkish dominion and turn it into the true successor to the Eastern Roman Empire of the Byzantines.

To understand the emergence of the Ottoman Turks as the successors to the Seljuks it is necessary to examine two phenomena, one arising from the nature of Turkish or Turkoman ideology and the other from Seljuk policy. The Turkish tribes who migrated into or towards Iran from the Central Asian steppes, a process which we have already noted in the context of the Seljuks, were converted to a form of Islam which they adopted with extreme fervour. At once they began to see themselves as involved in a holy war against those not converted, the unbelievers; and their own commanders assumed very much the character of holy warriors, ghazis. The ghazi tradition persisted among those Turks who found their way to Anatolia. While some members of the Seljuk ruling class, for example, might become extremely flexible in their theology as a result, perhaps, of the influence of urban civilisation, many of their nominal Seljuk subordinates, as well as the leaders of Turkish clans who did not share the Seljuk Ghuzz origins, declined to go down this path. The holy war, or jihad, was a

very real feature of the Islamic presence in Anatolia.

The second phenomenon arose from the very nature of Seljuk rule in Anatolia. The Seljuk Sultanate of Rum was only an outlying province of what had once been a vast empire stretching from the Mediterranean right across Syria, Mesopotamia and Iran to the rivers Oxus and Jaxartes and the shores of the Aral Sea. In other words, it was a frontier zone, a buffer between the Seljuk centre and the Christian front line represented by the Byzantines and their Crusader associates. The Turkish frontier barons could all too easily set up as rulers in their own right; and with the decline of Seljuk power in the 13th century, accelerated by pressure from the Il-Khan Mongols, this is exactly what happened. Rulers of many minor emirates arose both to contest power and territory with each other and to conduct, as good ghazis, war against the Byzantine infidel. It was in this environment that the polity of the Ottoman Turks was to emerge.

The post-Seljuk emirates of Anatolia which were particularly imbued with the ghazi conception occupied the western end of the Asia Minor Peninsula, where their rise was assisted by the near collapse of Byzantine power during the 13th century. The sacking of Constantinople by the Fourth Crusade in 1204 resulted not only in the plunder of much of Byzantium's wealth but also, for a while, in the division of the Empire into two competing parts. The Latins ruled in Constantinople until 1261, while the Greeks established a numbers of centres of opposition of which Nicaea (Iznik) became the most important. In 1261 the Byzantine Empire at Nicaea recaptured Constantinople, ushering in the era of the Emperors of the Palaeologus Dynasty who were to rule until the last Emperor of them all, Constantine XI, died at Turkish hands when the Ottomans finally took Constantinople in 1453.

The recovery of Constantinople by the Palaeologi did not mean the restoration of Byzantine unity, however. In 1204, just before the Latins had sacked Constantinople, the Comneni family, who had provided the Byzantine Imperial line from 1081 to 1185, captured the Black Sea port of Trabzon. This they proceeded to turn into the Empire of Trebizond and a rival centre of Byzantine power to the Latins, and then the Palaeologi, in Constantinople. The Trebizond Empire often followed a Turkish policy by no means parallel to that pursued in Constantinople. In the 1240s it became a tributary to the Il-Khan Mongols; and in the 14th and 15th centuries it was very closely involved in the non-Ottoman Turkish politics of its hinterland, the home of the Danishmendids and, later, of the Kara-Koyunlu ("Black Sheep") and Ak-Koyunlu ("White Sheep") Turks. There was to be more than one marriage alliance between the Comneni and the Ak-Koyunlu. Trebizond possessed important trade connections across the Black Sea to the states of the Caucasus and the shores of southern Russia, which gave access to the great overland route to China. Economic prosperity certainly helped Trebizond survive and in the event it outlasted Byzantium by some eight years, finally falling to the Ottomans in 1461. During its life of more than two and a half centuries the Empire of Trebizond was not of conspicuous assistance to its colleague Empire on the Bosphorus.

While in some respects the Palaeologi after 1261 did bring about a revival of Byzantium, they were unable to offer effective resistance to the continued advance of the Turks in western Anatolia. By 1300 Byzantine control had shrunk to little more than the Asian shore of the Sea of Marmara and the Bosphorus. It was inevitable that in the belt of ghazi emirates or beyliks, between what had once been the Seljuk heartland - now more or less under Mongol Il-Khan dominion - and the frontier along the coastal strip of the extreme west of the Anatolian peninsula to which the Byzantines were now clinging so desperately, some Turkish replacement to the Seljuks should begin to emerge. Nomad history worked that way; and great empires often began in the most obscure and humble circumstances. This was the case with the Ottomans (or Osmanlis).

The first Ottoman territory was situated between Dorylaeum (Eskişehir) and Nicaea (Iznik) where the followers of one Ertugrul had settled. The history of this group before Ertugrul is shrouded in mystery. It may have originated from the Kayi tribe of Turkomans who had migrated from northeastern Iran, perhaps in flight from Mongol invaders. It may, according to some historians, have had rather different origins. None of this is of great importance. What does matter is that in about 1280 AD Ertugrul was succeeded by his son Osman, who gave his name to the dynasty and who consolidated the control of the emirate and established its capital at Yenişehir, just to the northeast of the Byzantine stronghold of Bursa (Brusa). Bursa was the key to the southern shore of the Sea of Marmara. Its capture by Orhan, Osman's son, in 1326 while Osman lay on his deathbed, marked a giant step forward for the Ottoman dynasty. Bursa was soon to be turned into the Ottoman capital.

The rise of the Ottomans took place at a moment when the politics of Iran and adjacent regions were undergoing profound changes. The Il-Khan Dynasty, which for the second half of the 13th century directly or indirectly controlled the Sultanate of Rum, in the third decade of the 14th century suddenly began to disintegrate. War broke out between various branches of the Genghiskhanid family, the Il-Khans of Iran finding themselves in conflict with the Chagatai Khanate on the northeast. By 1327 the Il Khans had lost control of Anatolia; and a few years later their power in Iran collapsed. By the 1350s it had disappeared. On the eve of the Timurid invasion of Iran in the 1380s the country was the home of a number of weak and competing dynasties who were neither any barrier to the new Central Asian invader nor in a position to exercise any influence over the remote Turkish polities of the Byzantine borderlands.

Against this background, Orhan rapidly expanded the Ottoman dominions, so that by the time of his death in 1360 not only had they developed into a considerable state occupying the entire southern coast of the Sea of Marmara and a substantial hinterland (following the capture of the key towns of Nicaea or Iznik in 1331 and Nicomedia or Izmit some six years later), but they had expanded across the Dardanelles into the Gallipoli Peninsula and large portions of Thrace including the city of Adrianople (Edirne).

Orhan started to consolidate these European conquests by encouraging the physical emigration of Turks, along with their families, over the Straits into Europe where, no doubt, they found a significant Turkish population already established. Throughout the 11th century, for example, this area had been repeatedly invaded by bands of Pecheneg Turks who had migrated from Central Asia to the lower Danube. A number of Pecheneg tribes were converted to Christianity and permitted to remain in Byzantine territory, mainly in the Nis region of Serbia. They were followed by yet more Turks, like the Uzes (a group possessing the same Ghuzz or Oghuz origins as did the Seljuks) who turned up on the Danube in 1065: some Uzes were eventually settled in Macedonia. In the 1080s the Emperor Alexius Comnenus allowed a number of bands of Kipchak Turks (Cumans to the Byzantines) to establish themselves in lands to the south of the Danube.

By the time of Manzikert the Byzantine army, indeed, depended greatly upon Turkish recruits from the Balkans to meet the threat of Turkish invasion of Anatolia from the east; and in the years immediately after Manzikert it can be argued that the Byzantine Empire only managed to survive at all because it was able to call upon the aid of non-Muslim Turkish allies. In 1090-91, for example, the Seljuks attacked the Byzantine border in Anatolia both by land and sea, with armies threatening Nicomedia (Izmit) and the fleet blockading Smyrna (Izmir); and, to make matters worse, the Muslim Seljuk Turks were on this occasion joined by pagan Pecheneg Turks who approached Constantinople from Thrace, just as the Iranians and Avars had cooperated in the days of Heraclius. As Heraclius had been able to call upon the Khazars, so on this occasion Alexius Comnenus was able to summon Kipchak forces to help him beat off the Pecheneg threat.

There can be little doubt that these earlier Turkish arrivals in the Balkans, like the Pechenegs, Uzes and Kipchaks, found it easy enough to come to terms with the new Turkish presence brought about by Ottoman policies of conquest and settlement on the European side of the Straits, and to integrate themselves with the new arrivals. All three Turkish groups, for example, had arrived on the Byzantine borders still following the old shamanist cults of the ancestral steppes. Their exposure to Christianity had been both shallow and fairly brief: many experienced no great difficulty in accepting Islam.

The process of Turkification on the European side accelerated apace after Orhan's death in 1360 under Murad I when Turkish forces ranged over much of northern Greece, Serbia and Bulgaria. The Ottoman victory over the Serbs at Kossovo in 1389, the year of Murad's death, is one of the great turning points in European history. It brought Serbia's role as a major power in eastern Europe to an abrupt end and replaced it by that of the Ottoman Turks.

By 1389 the Ottoman state was already turning into an Empire, a rival to Byzantium. It straddled the waterway dividing Europe from Asia as Byzantium once had; and it had taken over many of the Byzantine Imperial cities on both sides. Its rulers had to consider not merely the government of their Turkish fellow tribesmen but also of numerous subject peoples who were neither Turkish nor Muslim. When Beyazit succeeded Murad in 1389 he was far more a Sultan than a ghazi warlord. Byzantine administrative practices relating to such matters as taxation had been adopted, and Christian slaves enrolled into the bureaucracy at highly responsible levels. The army, which was still central to the Ottoman state structure, while receiving floods of potential recruits from nomad Turkoman groups fleeing into Anatolia from the east before yet another Central Asian scourge, that of Timur (which in due course was to strike at the heart of Ottoman power), had under Murad begun to exploit the potential of recruits from the conquered Christian populations.

The Ottoman concentration upon Europe inevitably invited attack from Anatolia to their east, where other successor beyliks to the Seljuks did not observe with great enthusiasm this new power rising in the west. Beyazit had to look to Anatolia, where a powerful confederation was being organised against him under the leadership of the beylik of Karaman. By 1393 Bayezit was campaigning as far east as Kayseri, Çorum and Sinop, with raiding parties ranging even further, to Sivas and Erzincan.

These operations, however, took place in the shadow of a far greater danger than any posed by an Anatolian tribal chieftain. The Turkish conqueror from Central Asia, Timur, had reached the eastern edge of Anatolia in 1386 as part of his campaign in western Iran. In 1395 he appeared again on the Ottoman eastern flank, reaching Sivas before turning south to deal with what must have seemed to him more attractive targets like Aleppo, Damascus and Baghdad. The Ottomans, however, could not be ignored indefinitely: they constituted a thorn in the side of any power controlling both Mesopotamia and Iran. In 1402 Timur once more advanced into Anatolia where he annihilated Bayezit's army at Ankara, taking the Sultan prisoner.

Timur then sent raiding forces further west as far as Izmir (Smyrna); but he made no effort to convert western Anatolia into a permanent component of his empire. He had achieved his immediate objective, the elimination of an Ottoman threat on his extreme western flank. In any event, he died three years later in 1405; and the vigour of his empire did not long outlast him.

The battle of Ankara presented the Byzantines with an unexpected opportunity, jointly with allies in Western Christendom, to recover; not only had the Ottomans suffered a shattering defeat, but for more than a decade following it their state was divided by civil war over the disputed succession to Bayezit. Moreover, the power vacuum in Anatolia created both by the Timurid whirlwind and its abrupt departure, paved the way for the rise of two formidable Turkish confederations, those of the Ak-Koyunlu and Kara-Koyunlu Turks, to whom reference has already been made. From their origins, probably in the same Ghuzz background as the Seljuks, these two groups had established themselves by the time of the Timurid invasion in eastern Anatolia roughly in the area between Erzincan and Diyarbakir. By the 1430s, in the aftermath of Timur, they had created two impressive near empires, the Ak-Koyunlu in eastern Anatolia between Sivas and Lake Van, and the Kara-Koyunlu in Mesopotamia (including Baghdad) and northwestern Iran (including Tabriz and Kazvin). Eventually the two proto-empires were to be squeezed out of existence by the combined efforts of the Ottomans and the Safavids of Iran. Immediately after the Timurid disaster, however, they - and particularly the Ak-Koyunlu - could have been a very serious threat to the Ottomans had it been possible to combine their actions with those of the Christian states. The Ak-Koyunlu certainly appreciated the role of Christendom, at least in the shape of the Comneni of Trebizond, with whom their leaders had intermarried.

The Christians, however, failed to take any significant advantage of the situation. Within a few years Ottoman bands were once more wandering, apparently at will, through the remaining Byzantine hinterland, undistracted by any dangers from the east. The Sultan who achieved this revival was Mehmet I. His grandson, Mehmet II, had so built upon the pre-Timurid foundations of Bayezit that, in 1453, he was at last in a position to launch a successful assault on Constantinople itself.

In architectural terms the process of Ottoman expansion from domination of the southern shore of the Sea of Marmara to the final occupation of Constantinople can be seen in the two fortresses of Anadolu Hisari and Rumeli Hisari, which between them command the Bosphorus to the north of modern Istanbul. Anadolu Hisari was constructed on the Anatolian side of the Bosphorus by Bayezit in the 1390's just before the Timurid debacle to serve as an observation post overlooking Constantinople across the narrows. Rumeli Hisar was erected on the European shore by Mehmet as an essential preliminary to the encirclement of Constantinople; and with its completion, even before the Byzantine capital had fallen, the Ottomans controlled both banks of the waterways linking the Mediterranean with the Black Sea, a geopolitical role which Turkey has performed ever since.

The Rumeli Hisar, built by Sultan Mehmet II in four months in 1452, to isolate Constantinople from the Black Sea.

With the fall of Constantinople, the Ottoman Turks had finally come into their own as the heirs to the Eastern Roman Empire; but they faced formidable problems both in its administration and in the determination of its ultimate extent. In governing their conquest the Ottomans adopted a subtle and complex system which combined traditional Turkish practice developed during the period of the conflict between the Anatolian beyliks with, on the one hand,

Islamic law and, on the other, much of the governmental methods of the Byzantines. While many Christians had, under Ottoman rule, converted to Islam for a variety of reasons, conviction and relatively low taxation among them, yet Christian communities survived and, often flourished under the new dispensation. The Ottoman rulers had to find ways to combine toleration with Islamic orthodoxy.

They also had to devise means to exploit the manpower resources of their non-Muslim subjects. The Janissary system, with its roots in the old Islamic practice of creating slave armies, usually recruited from Turks, though in Egypt and North Africa there are many examples of such forces being based on black Africans. The institution was exploited by the Abbasid Caliphate as well as the Fatimids of Egypt; and many Turkish dynasties followed suit, not least with the Seljuk Sultanate of Rum. The concept of a slave army has no obvious western European parallel, and this is not the place to examine it in any detail. Suffice to notice that it could lead to the paradoxical consequence of the state actually being ruled by a class which was of servile status. The founder of the Delhi Sultanate at the very beginning of the 13th century, Qutb-ud-din, was a Turk with such a background. So also were the Mamluks (a term simply meaning slave; though not, it must be emphasised, of the domestic or household variety) who overthrew the Ayyubid dynasty in Egypt in the mid-13th century to replace it by a regime of rule by soldier-slaves of Turkish origin which persisted for over two and half centuries.

The Janissary system is of particular interest in that not only was it to play a major part in Ottoman administration but also it was to evolve into by far the most sophisticated version of the slave army. Already before 1453 the Ottomans had developed the institution common among Seljuk regimes to meet the new situation presented by the extensive conquests in the Christian Balkans. This involved the recruitment of Christian slave boys from the conquered peoples, mainly among Greeks and Slavs and in the form of a regularly and systematically assessed tribute, who were specially trained for the Sultan's service, not only as soldiers but also as administrators. Such Janissaries continued to form the nucleus both of elite regiments in the army and of the top cadres of the administration of the Ottoman empire right up to the 19th century. The system only ended in the crisis of 1826 when Mahmud II felt himself obliged to destroy it in a particularly ruthless manner so as to prevent the Janissaries taking over from the Ottoman Dynasty, just as the Mamluks had seized Egypt from the heirs of Saladin in the 13th century.

One symbol of the new status of the Ottoman regime was to be found in architecture. With the establishment of a capital at Bursa, and even more following its transfer to Edirne (Adrianople) in 1365 or 1366, the Sultans embarked upon a programme of construction of public buildings of which the mosques, with their domes and minarets, are the ones which most easily attract the attention of the modern traveller. This is in contrast to the less eye-catching baths, barracks and administrative offices, not to mention bridges and causeways and other utilitarian structures. Edirne even before the fall of Constantinople, saw the erection of some of the finest examples of Islamic architecture to be seen

anywhere; and in the 16th century it was the site for what is often thought to be Sinan's masterpiece, the Selimiye mosque. This use of architecture as a symbol of dominion, as well, of course, as of piety and public duty, was nothing new: as has already been remarked, it was just what Justinian did with the construction of Haghia Sophia in the 6th century. The Ottomans were to follow this path not only in Constantinople, which had by 1460 replaced Edirne as the capital, but also in the remoter parts of the empire, as witness, for example, the admirable Ali Pasha Mosque at Sarajevo in what is today Yugoslavia.

Drawing a limit to the new empire was no simple task. Just as Alexander of Macedon found that the liberation of the Ionian Greek city states in Anatolia almost inexorably led him to conquest in Central Asia and northwest India, so the Ottomans found that there was no such thing as an easily maintained frontier. From the outset they were under pressure from Europe where the Christian states, while singularly inept in concerted resistance to the Turkish advance, yet could not let it proceed unchecked. By the 1680s (the failure to capture Vienna in 1683 is a key date in this context) the European limits of the Ottoman empire stretched from the Dalmatian Coast on the Adriatic through Hungary (to include Budapest) into the depths of central Europe and the Ukraine to the edge of the Black Sea at the Crimea and the Sea of Azov. These frontiers reached in the middle of the 17th century were unstable in that they confronted the energetic process of evolution of European nation states; and from c.1683 onwards they were under constant attack. The 18th century saw the Russian expansion to the shores of the Black Sea, by which time most of Hungary and Transylvania had been lost to the Hapsburgs. Until the latter part of the 19th century, however, the Ottoman possessions in Europe (though some of them under Ottoman suzerainty rather than sovereignty) constituted one of the largest territorial blocks on that continent.

By 1453 the Ottomans had more than recovered from their defeat at Timur's hands in 1402, and the bulk of eastern Anatolia was in their hands. Mehmet added the final Greek stronghold in Asia, Trabzon (site of another Haghia Sophia, one of the very last great Byzantine churches), in 1461; and he also ended once and for all the threat of the beylik of Karaman (with its centre in the region of Konya), so that Ottoman territory now touched the Mediterranean on the Gulf of Iskenderun. These gains inevitably pushed the Ottomans into three directions, due east towards the Iranian Caucasus and Azarbaijan, southeastwards into the valleys of the Tigris and Euphrates towards Mesopotamia and the Persian Gulf, and, finally due south through Syria along the coastal strip leading to Egypt, the Red Sea and the northern African coast as far west as Algeria. By 1683 the Ottomans had advanced along all these avenues.

The course of the 16th century bestowed upon the Ottoman Empire a somewhat paradoxical character. It was clearly the successor to the Eastern Roman Empire - the occupation of Constantinople as its capital was reinforced by the fact that its territorial limits more or less coincided with Eastern Roman Imperial ambition -; yet, soon after the conquest of Egypt the Ottoman dynasty assumed for itself the Caliphate and the supreme command of Islam, thereby emphasising its challenge to the ideological values of those European nations who struggled to contain its advance. The title of Caliph, however, did not seem to be central to Ottoman policy.

By his Muslim subjects the Ottoman Sultan might be seen as Caliph, even if he did not make too much of this status and if there were legalistic doubts concerning his genealogical right to the title. Over the numerous non-Muslim subjects the Sultan was political lord without doubt, but, in spiritual matters often surprisingly tolerant. Non-Muslim minorities could flourish under the millet system which, in effect, left a great deal of authority to the heads of various ethnic and religious communities such as the Jews and the Greek Orthodox Christians. As a result of this policy there was considerable voluntary non-Muslim immigration into Ottoman territory, particularly during the 16th century. Sephardic Jews escaping persecution in Spain and Portugal found Turkish rule far more supportable than that of their Catholic Majesties. Peasants from many regimes adjacent to the Ottoman border found the Muslim side more congenial than the Christian.

The 16th century saw the beginning of what was to turn into a fatal flaw in the Ottoman structure, an inability to master the lines of communication of the sea. At first the Turks took to the water with surprising ability; and the Ottoman navy controlled the eastern Mediterranean in the first half of the 16th century. A turning point, however, was marked by the Turkish failure to capture Malta in 1565, followed shortly by the disastrous naval defeat of the Ottomans by a combined Venetian-Hapsburg fleet at Lepanto in 1571. These are famous events. Already, however, something more significant had taken place.

The Portuguese, who had found at the very end of the 15th century that it was possible to sail round Africa from the Atlantic to the Indian Ocean, in the first decade or so following the Ottoman capture of Egypt in 1517 challenged Turkish sea power at the entrance to the Red Sea; here they were not entirely successful, for they failed to deny Aden to the Ottomans. But by the middle of the century they had effectively denied to the Ottomans naval access to the open waters of the Indian Ocean, despite occasional Turkish forays from the Red Sea and the Persian Gulf to Gujerat in western India and down the east coast of Africa as far as Mombasa. The Ottoman regime was unable to exploit significantly the great potential of the ever expanding Asiatic maritime trade which has been such a feature of modern history: and at the moment of its greatest vitality it was, in effect, doomed to become ever more inward looking and isolated.

The Ottomans were rather more successful than their Byzantine and Roman predecessors in gaining control over Mesopotamia and an outlet to the Persian Gulf (though their maritime weakness prevented them from deriving the full benefit of this); but, like previous rulers of Anatolia, they faced a formidable foe in Iran. The revival of the Ottomans in Anatolia after the Timurid invasion is almost exactly

paralleled by the emergence of the Safavid line in Iran. The Safavids were native Iranian tribesmen rather than of Central Asian stock, and they originated from the northeastern corner of Iran in the neighbourhood of Ardebil in the mountains along the southwestern shore of the Caspian where today runs the border between Iran and the Soviet Union. Like the Ottomans they were confronted with the threat posed by the Ak-Koyunlu and Kara-Koyunlu Turkish confederations. Again like the Ottomans in their ghazi period, the Safavids acquired a religious purpose within Islam; but, unlike the Ottomans, it was directed towards the Sh'ia rather than the Sunni point of view. The rise of the Safavids assumed many of the aspects of a religious crusade in which the major opponents were Sunni Turkish tribal groups who controlled most of Iran in the Timurid aftermath.

Inevitably the Safavids of Iran also came into conflict with the Ottomans. The first crisis came in 1514, with the possession of Azarbaijan as the prize. Thenceforth Irano-Turkish war was almost constant. The Ottomans managed to extend their frontier right across the Caucasus to Baku and to acquire the whole of Persian Azarbaijan (including Tabriz), as well as Luristan. In the early 18th century however with both the Ottomans and the Safavids in decline, much of this territory was lost. By the end of the 18th century, with the exception of considerable territory in the Caucasus (most of which is now in the Soviet Union), the extreme eastern Ottoman frontier in Anatolia had become almost exactly what it is today, running between Lake Van on the Turkish side and Lake Urmia on the Iranian. Of course, in contrast to the present, there was added to all this a vast tract adjacent to the south of eastern Anatolia which included the Arab speaking lands of Syria, Palestine, Mesopotamia, Egypt and most of the Red Sea littoral of Arabia.

By the end of the 17th century the Ottoman Empire was very large indeed. This was an interesting moment in modern history when the Turks, with their close relatives the Mongols and the Tungus, ruled the greater part of the surface of the Eurasian landmass. From the northeastern frontier of Iran in Khorasan stretched eastwards a string of Turkish Khanates through Transoxiania into Eastern Turkestan where they reached the borders of the world of the Mongols and the Manchu Dynasty in China. In the 1690s the Manchus completed their subjugation of the Mongol tribes; and in the years that followed they extended their influence over the Turkish speaking peoples of Eastern Turkestan (which in the 1880s was to be converted into the Chinese Province of Sinkiang). In the late 17th century the Moghul Empire in India still seemed invincible and had conquered all but the extreme southern tip of the subcontinent. It is perfectly legitimate, in the context of world history, to speak of this as the age of the Turko-Mongol-Tungus just as the 19th century became the age of the dominance of western Europe.

Why, then, did the Ottoman imperial structure decline so drastically during the 19th century and disappear in the first decades of the 20th century? The Ottomans during the course of the 19th century made very great efforts to reform themselves. The so-called tanzimat period which began in 1839 witnessed serious endeavours to modernise the bureaucratic structure of the Ottoman state and endow it with some form of representative institutions. The Dynasty was, of course, under enormous pressures, from the European Powers, from rising nationalisms like that which had resulted (with European help) in the loss of Greece, and from the challenge posed by other modernising Islamic polities such as Egypt, nominally part of the Ottoman Empire but effectively independent from the beginning of the century.

Constitutional reform of the Ottoman Empire during the 19th century rather encouraged nationalist separatism on the part of the non-Turkish peoples than assisted the Empire in maintaining its integrity. This was, in fact, inevitable; and it was paralleled by analogous movements in other Empires of the period, that of the Hapsburgs perhaps offering the best example. No amount of devising of constitutions could hold together a multi-national empire of the kind which the Ottomans had created in the face of the nationalist ideas of the 19th century. It is surprising that the Ottomans did so well in delaying the inevitable.

Probably the greatest external pressure which confronted the Ottoman regime in the 19th century came from the expanding Empire of Tsarist Russia. Once the Russian dominions had reached the shores of the Black Sea, as they did in the last years of the 18th century (culminating in the Russo-Turkish Treaty of Jassy of 1791 which confirmed Russian possession of the Crimea and the entire littoral of the Sea of Azov as well as the coastal tract between the Bug and Dniestr Rivers in which was to rise the great port of Odessa), it was inevitable that Russian policy should be directed towards gaining free access to the Mediterranean through the Bosphorus and the Dardanelles and thus to challenge the very existence of Ottoman power which had its geopolitical basis in the control of that waterway.

The Russians, like the alliance of Sassanian Iranians and Avars in the 7th century AD, aproached the core of the Ottoman state, Anatolia and Thrace, in a giant pincer movement. On the one hand was the steady Tsarist advance into the Caucasus leading to the annexation of the Kars region in 1878, and the advance into eastern Anatolia during World War I which was aborted by the outbreak of the Russian Revolution (which, incidentally, also brought Kars back under Turkish rule). On the other hand there was Russian involvement in the affairs of the Balkans which brought the Tsarist army almost to the gates of Istanbul in 1829 following the capture of Edirne, and again during the Balkan crisis of 1877-78. In 1915 the Allies agreed to let Russia have Constantinople after the War, an agreement from the implementation of which only the Russian Revolution saved them.

Russian pressure was a major factor in forcing the Ottomans to involve themselves in the international politics of Europe. The Ottoman Empire became to all intents and purposes one of the European Powers and part of the European system of alliances. When the Ottomans declared war on Russia in late 1853 other Powers were inextricably involved; and by the following year the Turks were fighting alongside Britain, France and Sardinia in the Crimean War. This diplomatic dimension (by no means novel to the Ottomans who, for example, had enjoyed a special relationship with France set out in a Franco-Turkish treaty of as long ago as 1536) brought short term advantages. In the long run, however, it embroiled the Ottoman Empire in the great European conflict of 1914-18 with disastrous results.

The outbreak of World War I precipitated a crisis that would have come sooner or later. Defeat in 1918 resulted for the time being in the disintegration of the Ottoman Empire which, despite its European losses between the 1870s and 1913, was still very substantial in Asia; and it very nearly brought about a partition of the Turkish heartland which would have left the Ottoman Sultan ruling as a puppet in Constantinople under the watchful supervision of the British, French and Italians, not to mention the Greeks. Naturally, there were Turkish patriots who refused to be reconciled to a future of this kind.

For those who were not prepared to accept the plans of the victorious Allies for the former Ottoman Empire as fait accompli there were three possible lines of political thinking. First, the dream might still be entertained that the old Empire could somehow be revived. In the face of Arab reactions to Ottoman rule during the War this was, to say the least, unrealistic. Second, it was possible to see in the chaos following the War, and particularly as a consequence of the disturbances in Central Asia arising from the Russian Revolution, that it might be possible to create some kind of federation of Turkish states, or, at least, channel nationalist energies into assisting the achievement of independence by Turks outside the former limits of the Ottoman Empire. It is interesting in this context that Enver, one of the leading figures of the Young Turk movement, ended his days in Central Asia engaged on enterprises related to such a line of reasoning. Third, it might be possible to save out of the chaos of defeat not the Ottoman Empire but a Turkish state based on the old Turkish heartland of Anatolia.

This third view was that held by Mustafa Kemal Atatürk; and it was this view that was to give rise to the modern Turkish Republic. In one way it was revolutionary, a radical departure from the past as well as a challenge to opposing circumstances of the time. In another way, however, the Atatürk Revolution represented a thread in Turkish history that can be traced back a long time. Atatürk's policy of bringing about fundamental cultural, social, political and economic change for the peoples of the Turkish core, Asia Minor and Turkish Thrace, was certainly dramatic; but the changes involved were probably no greater than those undergone by the Seljuk Turks during the course of the 11th century AD. Atatürk's abandonment of imperial vision and concentration upon the Turkish heartland as the extent of the territory of the new Turkey was, again, a departure from Ottoman precedents; but it involved the acceptance of a political reality which had been capable of detection in the pages of eastern Mediterranean history since at least the days of Darius the Achaemenian. Certainly, by the time of the Timurid incursion of 1402 the present extent of the Turkish Republic, Anatolia plus a foothold on the other side of the Bosphorus and Dardanelles in order both to protect the western flank and to control communications between the Mediterranean and the Black Sea, had acquired a geopolitical logic of considerable force; and this, without doubt, Atatürk acknowledged when he moved the new Turkish capital to Ankara, near the centre of Anatolia as well as being the site of Timur's great victory.

In the immediate post-1918 years there was further replay, so to speak, of the ancient history of the eastern Mediterranean which demonstrated another aspect of the Anatolian past. Just as in Turkish eyes Anatolia has long been a heartland, so in the vision of some Greek nationalists it was perceived as that crucial hinterland to the Hellenic world of the eastern Mediterranean. The war between the Greeks, invading Anatolia, and the Turkish nationalists of which Atatürk was the leading figure, echoes in some ways the old contest between the Greek city states and the ruler of the Anatolian plateau, the Great King; or, even of more distant struggles between the Hittites and the kings of Arzawa. Thanks to the genius of Atatürk and the determination of his soldiers the Anatolian side won and a new Turkey was born.

The Turkish Republic, which formally came into being on 29th October 1923, departed in many crucial ways from the pattern of the Turkish past. It was non-imperial and, above all, it was secular. One of Atatürk's first actions as President of the new state was to bring about, in March 1924, the abolition of the Caliphate (even though Islam continued for a while to be recognised as the official Turkish religion). In its territorial extent, however, it was as we have already noted, following a number of impressive precedents accumulated over four thousand years of history.

There is a temptation to look upon Turkey as a kind of museum where the Turks are the curators of the relics of the past of many other unrelated peoples. This is not the case. An immensely strong chain of historical continuity links the Turkey of today to this great wealth of physical remains of past regimes, epochs and cultures.

One purpose of this book is to display some of these treasures in their contemporary surroundings as they may be seen by a traveller today. For those who have seen the richness of this country, it may refresh their memories; and for those who have yet to visit Turkey, it may encourage them to go and see for themselves.

The columns of the Temple of Artemis at Sardis.

CHAPTER I

ISTANBUL AND THE BOSPHORUS

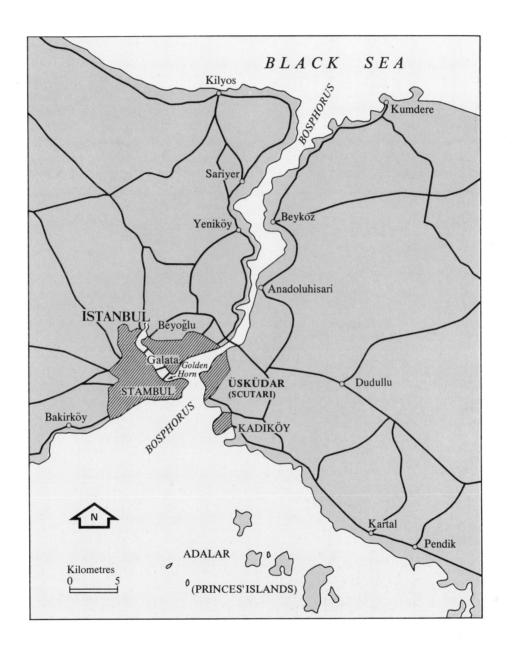

It is not possible in a single chapter to do more than glimpse at a few of the wonders of this extraordinary city. Founded in the 7th century BC by Byzas the Megarian, the city was no more than a strategically placed way-station en route to the Black Sea. Constantine changed this in 330 AD when he moved the seat of Empire from unruly Rome. In the next millennium and a half the city was the focal point of Empire, first Byzantine and then Ottoman.

Today the city is greatly enlarged, and is the only city in the world that sits astride two Continents. The glory and the beauty remain undimmed. The waters around Istanbul contrive to give it an added dimension.

Opposite: The Galata Tower

Writing in the middle of the 19th century, Julia Pardoe records the following. "A novel feature in the Golden Horn is the floating-bridge by which it is spanned and which has been constructed within the last three years. It is flung across the harbour from the ferry of Galata, and is a great and commodious means of communication with the opposite shore. Two rather lofty arches admit the passage of small craft beneath the bridge, which is singularly elegant in its design."

Today the double-tiered bridge, built in 1909-12 to replace the wooden floating-bridge, is the focal point of Istanbul's colourful daily life. There is a constant stream of pedestrians and traffic in both directions. The centre of the bridge pivots at 04.00 each day to allow large ships through. It is more than just a bridge, for on the lower tier there are shops of every description, tea-houses and restaurants. Fishing from the lower tier is a common and soothing distraction from the bustle above.

During the 11th century the Byzantines granted commercial concessions to the various Italian trading city-states such as Venice, Amalfi, Pisa and Genoa. The first three were given strips of land along the Golden Horn where they could build docks and warehouses. The Genoese were granted much of Galata across the water on the hill of Pera. At first the Byzantines derived some benefit from these concession areas, but with time they became independent principalities, ruled from their home cities in Italy. This was particularly true in Galata, where the Genoese built massive walls, a moat, and, most impressive of all, the Galata Tower. The tower was important both as the apex of the defence system and as a lookout for merchant ships sailing into the Bosphorus. To gain an impression of the isolation of Galata from the mainstream of Constantinople life, it is helpful to remember that Galata was unaffiliated and neutral during the siege and fall of Constantinople in 1453. Later the tower fell into disrepair, and was rebuilt by the Ottomans as a fire-watch tower. Today the tower houses a good restaurant and provides marvellous views across the Golden Horn. There is no better place to gain a panoramic view of Istanbul and its magnificent skyline.

Over, pages 36/37: View across the Golden Horn from the Galata Tower.

Above: The floating-bridge across the Golden Horn (Pardoe and Bartlett, 1839).

Above: The skyline of Istanbul, the Galata Tower right.

Above: The modern Galata Bridge, with the Galata Tower behind.

The Sultan Ahmet Mosque dominates the skyline of Istanbul with its six minarets and shows clearly in every engraving, painting and photograph of the city in the past three hundred and fifty years. It was begun in 1609 on the orders of Sultan Ahmet I and completed eight years later. Its exterior is the most beautiful of all the imperial mosques in Istanbul, with its many domes and semi-domes blending to form a harmonious whole. It is unusual for a mosque to have more than four minarets. Contemporary detractors of Sultan Ahmet accused him of lack of piety, saying that only at Mecca were there more than four minarets to a mosque. This was patently false, for there were seven at the great mosque at Basra.

For several centuries it was the mosque where the Sultan performed his Friday prayers. This was because of its proximity to Topkapi Sarayi, the imperial palace. The formal processions to and from the mosque were a splendid ritual spectacle.

Opposite: The Sultan Ahmet Mosque from the air.

Below: The Sultan Ahmet Mosque from the Hippodrome (Allom and Walsh, 1838).

Above: Detail of the ceiling of a
semi-dome, Sultan Ahmet Mosque.

Opposite: Prayers in the Sultan
Ahmet Mosque.

The Haghia Sophia is one of the world's most important buildings architecturally, and its history is appropriately dramatic. The present building is the third church to stand on this site. The first was roughly similar in size, and it was known as the Great Church. Built in the reign of Constantius, son of Constantine the Great, it was completed in 360 and dedicated to Haghia Sophia, the Divine Wisdom, an attribute of Christ. This first church was destroyed by fire in 404 during a riot. A new church was built by Theodosius II, but this was also burnt down in 532 during the Nika Revolt. Justinian the Great had work begun on the present church in the same year, and it was completed in 537, under the supervision of Anthemius of Tralles and Isidore of Miletus, both 6th century mathematical geniuses.

The newly built church had a huge but very shallow dome, and after several earthquakes part of it collapsed in 558. The original architects were dead by now, so the work of rebuilding was entrusted by Justinian to the architect's nephew, Isidore the Younger. The new dome was less shallow, and therefore suffered from fewer lateral stresses, but nevertheless there was a further collapse in 988 after earthquakes in the 9th and 10th centuries. The dome was again rebuilt, this time with Trdat the Armenian as architect. Serious damage was done to the church during the Latin sack of Constantinople in 1204 (the Fourth Crusade), and the dome collapsed yet again in 1346. It was reconstructed by 1355; but during the last century of Byzantine rule the church fell into disrepair, as did much of the city.

The last Christian service was held in the evening of 28th May 1453. The Emperor Constantine XI Dragases came with his Greek and Italian knights to offer a prayer for the city; but within hours the walls had been breached and the city fell to the Ottomans. Sultan Mehmet II rode directly to the church, and ordered it to be converted into a mosque. The Sultan and his successors restored the building to its former greatness, and it never again was allowed to fall into disrepair. There have been periodic restorations, and in 1934 it was opened as a museum.

To stand in the Haghia Sophia is to be witness to sixteen hundred years of history. The impressions of space, grandeur and the magnificence of another age are overwhelming.

Above: Haghia Sophia from the air.

Above: The huge central dome of Haghia Sophia.

Above: Turks from the country admiring the Haghia Sophia.

Topkapi Sarayi was for more than four hundred years the imperial residence of the Ottoman Sultans. The last century of Byzantine rule saw a sad decline of Constantinople; many of its public buildings fell into disrepair as the population shrank, and the palaces of the emperors were no exception. So in 1453 the conqueror Sultan Mehmet II had to start from scratch. After a false start in the centre of the peninsula he decided to build on the hill nearest the main waterway, the site of the acropolis of ancient Byzantium. He began by building a huge wall around the acropolis. The main sea-gate in this wall was called Topkapi, the Cannon Gate, from two enormous cannon that flanked it, and it eventually gave its name to the whole complex. Palace buildings were built on the high ground, and parks and gardens on the slopes. This was during the period 1459-65. Many fires and

rebuildings and additions have occurred over the centuries, but in essence the Topkapi complex is not much changed from the 15th and 16th centuries.

Topkapi was not just the private residence of the Sultan and his Court. As home of the Divan it was the seat of the supreme executive and of judicial control of a great empire. Here the fate of nations was decided. Moreover it housed the most select school for training for the imperial civil service.

Today, out of season, its gardens and courtyards grant peace from the bustle and the traffic of the city. And in its rooms are housed the most astonishing collections of rare objects which once belonged to the sultans.

Below: The domes and chimneys of Topkapi Sarayi.

Left: The Pavilion of the Holy Mantle, Topkapi Sarayi.

Below: The main gate, Bab-i Humayun, of Topkapi Sarayi.

The Süleimaniye Mosque is a splendid monument to its splendid founder, Suleiman the Magnificent. It is the finest of all the imperial mosques and the most important Ottoman building in the city. Begun in 1550, the mosque itself was completed in 1557, although the subsidiary buildings of the complex took some further years to complete.

The exterior of the mosque impresses by its scale; it is the interior which takes one's breath away with its simple beauty. Many of the greatest Ottoman artists combined their work to produce one of the architectural masterpieces of the world. The incomparable Sinan was the architect; the marvellous stained glass windows are by the glazier Sarhoş Ibrahim, better known as Ibrahim the Drunkard; the superb inscriptions throughout the mosque are by that most renowned of Ottoman calligraphers, Ahmet Karahisari and his famous pupil Hasan Çelebi. And the tiles, sparingly used, were the first from the new Iznik kilns of the 16th century. The marble and wood work are also of the highest order. The overall effect is magnificent.

Above: Interior of the Süleimaniye Mosque (Pardoe and Bartlett, 1839).

Above: Domes and half-domes of the Süleimaniye Mosque.

In the 1840's the Ottomans established a weaving centre of excellence at Hereke to weave carpets, and especially silk carpets, for the royal palaces. Superb works have been produced ever since, and the name Hereke is synonymous with the highest quality.

Left: A modern Hereke carpet.

Above and left: Weaving of fine carpets continues today at Hereke.

For most of its history the vast majority of Istanbul's houses were built of wood. Inevitably this led to fires on a grand scale, which sometimes lasted for weeks. Edicts were published to encourage building in stone, but there were too few craftsmen or rich customers to change the habits of centuries. Only in modern times has the city turned away from wood for its buildings. Today these wooden houses are rare. Along the Bosphorus they lend a pleasant 19th century air to their surrounds.

Left and below: Wooden houses by the Bosphorus, in the 19th century and today.

Istanbul sits astride two continents. It has for two thousand years been a centre of communications and trade, both by sea through the narrows and by land across them. Little changes. But in this century the railway and road links across the Bosphorus have been added.

Left: The Bosphorus Bridge, opened in 1973, the fourth longest suspension bridge in the world.

Below: Istanbul's railway terminus on the Asian side of the Bosphorus. Note the ferries for carrying trains.

Surrounded by architectural masterpieces of many ages, the
life of the city goes on as it has always done. For two
thousand years men have been selling fruit and vegetables,
meat and fish in the same way in the same places.

Opposite: Fish sellers by the Galata
Bridge.

Below: Fruit and vegetable market,
Istanbul.

Above: Gateway of Istanbul University.

Left: Bookshop in Sahaflar Çarşisi, near the Covered Bazaar.

Left: Card players in a courtyard off the Covered Bazaar.

The great Covered Bazaar of Istanbul was first built in 1461. It has suffered from fire (most recently in 1954) and earthquake on numerous occasions, but has usually been rebuilt more or less as it was. As in any old market the trades are clustered together, often on a single street. The scale and atmosphere are unique.

Below: View of the great Covered Bazaar of Istanbul (Allom and Walsh 1838).

Edirne was founded by the Emperor Hadrian in 125 AD and for long was known by his name, Adrianople. It has witnessed many great battles. In 323 Constantine the Great won a victory here on his march to Byzantium. Even more significantly, the Emperor Valens was killed here when the Goths overwhelmed his Roman army in 378, thereby opening the Eastern frontier to ravage and turmoil. In 811 the Emperor Nicephorus I was killed at Adrianople by the Bulgars; his skull was made into a goblet for a victory feast. During the next five hundred years the town was repeatedly fought over, by Byzantines, Avars, Bulgars, Crusaders and finally Turks.

Left: Courtyard of the Selimiye Mosque complex.

Below: The Selimiye Mosque at sunset.

Above: Dome of the Selimiye Mosque.

Edirne became the capital of the expanding Ottoman Empire for nearly a century, until the fall of Constantinople. After 1453 it remained a favourite home of the Sultans, who adorned it with many splendid buildings. But the last two centuries have been hard on Edirne. Occupied and ravaged by the Russians in 1829 and 1878, by the Bulgars in 1913 and by the Greeks in 1919-22, it has declined into a quiet and pleasant market town.

Edirne's claim to fame is not, however, as a battlefield. For it was here, in 1569-75, that the great architect Sinan built what he regarded as the masterpiece of his career. The Selimiye Mosque may be considered the supreme achievement of Ottoman architecture, surpassing even the Süleymaniye of Istanbul in its beauty and grandeur.

The Ottomans were patrons of many arts and skills, among them ceramics. Tiles for any new and important Ottoman mosque were designed in Istanbul by artists working under the supervision of a "director of faience". The designs were then sent to Iznik for execution. Iznik had been destroyed in 1402 by Timur; however within a century the ancient city had revived (see page 228), and under the patronage of successive Ottoman Sultans a considerable tile industry grew up. Several hundred tile factories and kilns existed in the 16th century, and the best of Ottoman faience work came from this centre.

Opposite: Tiles and the mihrab of the Mosque of Rustem Paşa, one of the most beautiful of the smaller mosques of Sinan, built in 1561. The tiles come from the kilns of Iznik, then at its zenith. Note the tulips, a favourite Ottoman theme.

THE ANATOLIAN PLATEAU AND THE BLACK SEA

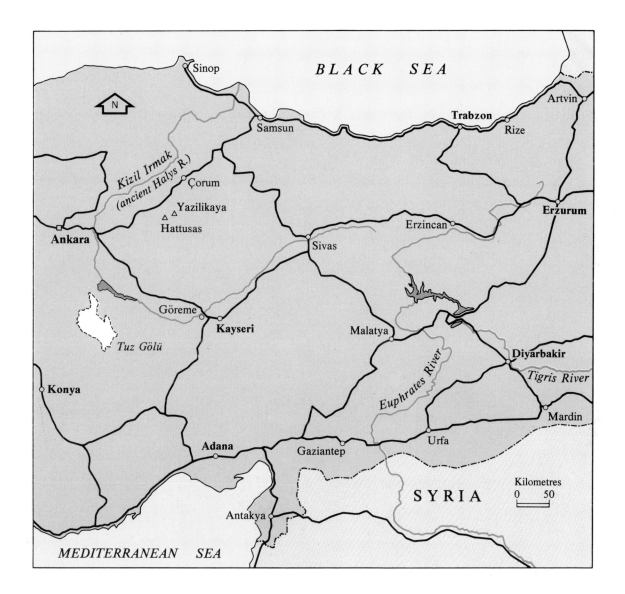

The Anatolian Plateau, with its wide spaces and huge skies, contrasts with the Black Sea coastline, where wooded mountainsides crowd the sea. The Plateau's climate is dry and hard; the Black Sea's wet and soft. Both regions have long histories, often violent, always interesting.

Opposite: Mosque at Kalecik, east of Trabzon, Black Sea behind.

Ankara has a long history, under various names, for it was well placed on the major ancient trade routes and was defensible because of its many hills. But it was only a town of 30,000 inhabitants when in 1919 Atatürk moved his headquarters there. Later he decided on it as Turkey's new capital.

In Hittite times its name was Ankuwash, and it was on the Royal Road from Hattusas to Sardis. In the late 3rd century BC Pergamum defeated the Gauls who had come to Asia Minor as mercenaries but had then tried to carve out a place for themselves. They were settled in old Phrygia, and the area around Ankara became Galatia. It was an important trading town under the Romans. The Byzantines knew it as Ankyra, the Seljuks as Enguriye. Later prosperity came with the Angora goat, and as Angora it was known in the 19th century and up to 1919. Today it is a busy capital city of nearly 3 million inhabitants.

Opposite: Street scene in downtown Ankara.

Below: A view from the Citadel over old Ankara to the modern city below.

In 1927 Atatürk addressed the youth of Turkey with an exhortation which began as follows:

> "Turkish Youth! Your very first duty is to defend and protect Turkish freedom and the Turkish Republic until eternity."

The full text is found in Turkish on the wall of the Ministry of National Education, Ankara.

Above: Atatürk's exhortation on the wall of the Ministry of National Education.

Periodically in history a genius emerges who is able to alter the course of events for a whole nation. Atatürk was such a man. Almost single-handed he created modern Turkey from the ashes of the Ottoman dynasty. It is fitting that the whole Turkish nation reveres his memory.

Above: The Atatürk Mausoleum, Ankara.

The Anatolian Plateau is a huge high plateau, bounded on three sides by mountains and on the west by a fallaway to the valleys of the Aegean. In places there is a flat steppe country, especially around Konya. But more usual is undulating ground, with large horizons.

The climate is a typical continental climate of extremes, hot and dry in summer, bitterly cold in winter. The average altitude is between 1000 and 1500 metres, so it is never suffocatingly hot. But the cold in winter, especially in high places such as Kars and Erzurum in the east, can be desperate. The villages and towns are built pragmatically, to withstand the elements.

Above: A rebuilt han at Kayseri.

Above and below: Plateau village.

Kayseri, as one might expect from its exposed position on
the Anatolian Plateau, has had a very chequered history.
The settlement of the area dates back at least to Hittite times,
but Kayseri only emerged from the mists of antiquity as the
capital of a Cappadocian Kingdom in the 4th century BC. It
was an important Roman frontier town and was renamed
Caesarea. Over the centuries it was successively held by the
Sassanian Persians, the Seljuks, the Mongols, and
independent Turkish beys; it was the second Seljuk city after
Konya. It was finally brought into the Ottoman Empire in
1515.

Below: The Ahmet Paşa Mosque
at Kayseri, built in 1585, with the
snows of Erciyes Dag (3916
metres) behind.

The open plains and rolling hills of the Anatolian Plateau
have always made it excellent cavalry country, and its history
of an endless succession of mounted invaders reflects this.
The wind, even in spring, can be piercingly cold. The overall
impression on the plateau is of space and sky.

Below: Plateau village in spring.

About four million years ago eruptions of nearby volcanos such as Hasan Dag and Erciyes Dag deposited huge volumes of volcanic ash. These eruptions were followed by lava flows which capped the soft volcanic ash. Four million years of weathering has differentially eroded these soft and hard rocks. Where hard rock remains to 'protect' the soft ash below, unusual cones and pinnacles of soft tufa remain, crowned by the hard lava. These are the "Chimneys of Angels" of Cappadocia.

Although a Kingdom as early as 600 BC, Cappadocia was never an identifiable nation. But the people of the area early found that the soft tufa was easily excavated. The result was homes and storerooms and eventually, with the coming of Christianity, churches and monastic communities. The scenery of Cappadocia is almost lunar in its beauty.

Even more extraordinary are the underground cities. Six have been discovered to date, and there may be more. The deepest goes down fifteen floors, with air shafts down to 400 feet. One covers nine square kilometres. Moreover the cities are interconnected by very long tunnels. No mention is made of them in any classical history or geography, yet a Roman tomb has been found in one and a Hittite-style grain mill in another. Clearly they were for refuge from the frequent raids and invasions Cappadocia has always been subject to. Whole populations must have literally disappeared at the approach of an invader.

Below: The town of Ürgüp, amid the pinnacles and caves of Cappadocia.

Above and below: Cave-homes in the soft volcanic tufa, near Göreme.

Above, below and opposite: Typical Cappadocian scenery, near Göreme.

Left: Procession of Hittite Gods at Yazilikaya, near Boğazköy.

It was not until this century, with the starting in 1905 of the excavations at Boğazköy, that the references in the Old Testament and in various ancient inscriptions to the Hittites were put in context and the full extent of the Hittite Empire and its legacy to civilisation was understood. For these are the ruins of Hattusas, the capital of an empire that lasted for six hundred years (18th to 12th centuries BC), ruling from the Aegean to Mesopotamia, and that possessed a civilisation which would leave its mark on all later Anatolian cultures.

Below: Hittite carvings in a rock chamber at Yazilikaya, near Boğazköy.

Left: Huge well-fitting stones in a wall at Boğazköy.

The Hittites arrived at Hattusas (the capital of the Hatti, their predecessors) around 2000 BC. For the next eight centuries Hattusas developed from a City-State (2000-1750 BC) to the centre of a Kingdom (1750-1450 BC) to the capital of a great Empire (1450-1180 BC).

There is much to see at Hattusas. The best of the Hittite artefacts are in the Museum at Ankara, but this ancient site evokes an atmosphere of simple grandeur and immense power.

Below: General view of the Hittite capital at Boğazköy.

Sumela Monastery, 54 km south of Trabzon, high in the wooded mountains, was founded in the 6th century AD. It is perched impressively inside a huge cave on a towering cliff.

The monastery was continuously inhabited for thirteen centuries, until 1923. It was restored at various times. But alas it gradually fell into disrepair; neglect and a fire have reduced this once splendid monastery to a ruin; but a ruin which for its marvellous site, its history and its damaged frescoes is well worth visiting.

Above: Fresco showing Jonah and the Whale, Sumela.

Below: Sumela Monastery from below.

Right: The Ayia Sophia, Trabzon.

Below: Interior of the Ayia Sophia, Trabzon.

Some three kilometres from Trabzon is one of the most evocative Byzantine buildings in Anatolia. The Ayia Sophia was built in the mid 13th century as a monastery church, but of all the monastic buildings only the church has survived. After 1461 it was used as a mosque, with the wall paintings covered over with whitewash. Now it is a museum.

The marvellous wall paintings have been restored and give an excellent impression of the late 13th century Byzantine traditions. Visit the church in the afternoon, with the late sun giving a special light to these ancient paintings, and it is impossible not to be deeply moved.

The Black Sea coast contrasts with the rest of Turkey. Here the mountains fall directly into the sea, leaving space for a village or town only at the mouths of rivers or streams. The climate is wet and soft. The hills are covered with trees and vegetation, and the rivers abound with trout. Much tea is grown around Rize. No wonder Xenophon's mercenaries gave a shout of triumph when they crossed the last crest above Trabzon and saw the sea.

Opposite: Boat building in the old way at Of, near Rize, on the Black Sea. Of, with its splendid name, was famous for producing fanatical bishops who indulged in acrimonious doctrinal disputes.

Below: A farmhouse in the Black Sea foothills.

Right: Tea picking near Rize.

Opposite: A cattle market at Çayeli, east of Rize.

Below: Black Sea scenery, looking up from the coast to terraces of tea and hidden mosques.

CHAPTER III

THE NORTH-EAST: BEYOND ERZURUM

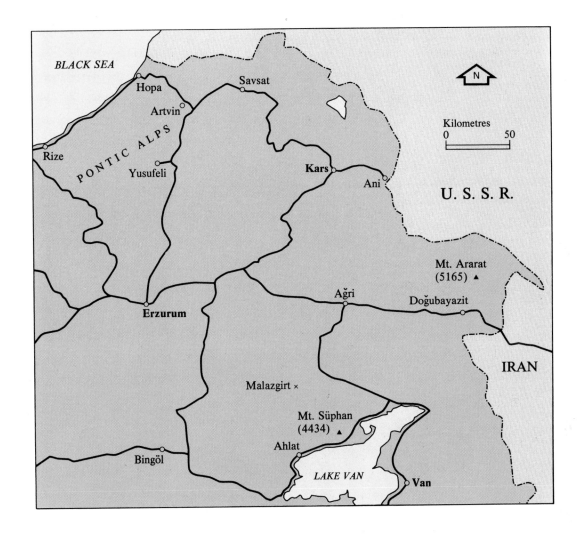

To the ancients this region was the roof of the world. With altitudes beginning at 1600 metres and going as high as Mount Ararat's 5165 metres, it is not surprising to find long bitter winters with much snow and biting winds. But come in the other seasons, and especially in May and June, and the country is welcoming.

The variety is astonishing. The deep valley gorges of the Pontic Alps contrast with the wider spaces of the upper plains: and over all broods the immensity of Ararat.

Opposite: Camp at the foot of the Greater Kaçkar (3937 metres) in the Pontic Alps.

The valleys to the south and east of Artvin are precipitous gorges, with villages perched high above on the mountainside. This is the land of the Georgians. It is rich with marvellous fruit and long uphill walks. There are 10th and 11th century churches and castles on inaccessible spires of rock. The Georgians called themselves Kartveli, and they were already here early in the first millennium BC, for they are referred to by Assyrian and Urartian inscriptions. But the Persians called them Gurj, and so we have Georgia. The many invaders of Anatolia generally left these mountain people to themselves, for the gorges were virtually impregnable. It was not until Ottoman times that the region was fully incorporated into an empire.

Opposite: Village of Tek Kale, near Yusufeli.

Below: Church and castle on a rocky pinnacle, Tek Kale near Yusufeli.

Seventy kilometres east of Artvin lies Şavşat, once the chief town of a Georgian province. Above the town the mountain gorges are left behind and the country is rolling and verdant. The houses are almost Alpine in their construction, and the fields and the hills give a marvellous feeling of space. Here is surely a place to hire a horse and explore the country as it should be explored.

Opposite: Rolling hills and farmland, above Şavşat.

Below: Summer grazing log cabins, above Şavşat.

Kars, at 1750 metres, has as hard and long a winter as any place in Turkey. It first appears in history as an Armenian town in the 8th century AD, but there may have been a much earlier Urartian settlement here; for Kars occupies a strategic position at the mouth of a gorge and its very name means gate. Behind are the green and valuable grazing uplands. It has changed hands many times in the last thousand years, notably in 1855, in a sideshow to the Crimean War, when a Turkish garrison led by a British general held out gallantly for months against overwhelming odds. It was again Russian between 1878 and the end of the First World War.

Left: The Kars region is famous for its geese.

Opposite: The Citadel at Kars, scene of so many sieges.

Below: The uplands beyond Kars.

Right on the frontier with Russia, roughly an hour beyond Kars, lies the ancient Armenian capital of Ani. Permission is required to visit Ani, and should be obtained at Kars; photography is forbidden, for the Russians are very sensitive watchers of all visitors to this wonderful site.

Ani is on a high plateau. On two sides flow deep-gorged rivers; the third side of the triangle of Ani was protected by walls more than a kilometre long. Ani was founded in the 9th century on a site which even then dated back three thousand years. In the 10th century it became the Armenian capital and it was then that many of the superb churches were built. At its height the city boasted a population of between 100,000 and 200,000. But the medieval history of the Armenian nation was one of turmoil, and more than once the city was overwhelmed by invaders. Thirteenth century Mongol raids and a fourteenth century earthquake of terrible severity put an end to Ani's greatness. In the early fifteenth century conquest by Timur emptied the city. For five hundred years it was lost to history, to be rediscovered by 19th century travellers. They found it as we see it today, desolate and empty, with the remaining buildings like wrecks on a beach.

Below: General view of Ani (Brosset, 1860).

Opposite: The 13th century Church of St.Gregory, Ani (photographed by Lynch, 1901).

If you are driving along the main Turkish-Iranian highway, it is all too easy to drive past one of the most extraordinary buildings in Turkey, the Ishak Paşa Sarayi. Built on a platform with a marvellous view over the Ararat plain, this unusual palace was the inspiration of a dynasty of local overlords in the second half of the 18th century. Ishak Paşa, who was created overlord in 1789, ruled over eastern Anatolia under nominal Ottoman sovereignty. From this fortress he dominated the trade which flowed along the Silk Road below (virtually the same route as the highway follows today), gaining much wealth and spending it on the creation of this palace.

The architecture makes the palace exotically unique. For the architect has borrowed from the Seljuk, Persian, Georgian, Armenian and Ottoman styles, and brought them all together in one complex. The juxtapositions may surprise, but the overall effect is strangely pleasing. Of special note are the acoustics of the mosque, which are worth experimenting with; the view from the minaret; and design and position of the main water closet. Overall a fantastic fortress.

Behind is an ancient Urartian citadel, with later Seljuk and Ottoman walls; and below the remains of the old town. The climb to the citadel is worthwhile, if only for the best overall view of Ishak Paşa's whimsy.

Preceding pages: The complex of buildings of Ishak Paşa Sarayi near Doğubeyazit.

Below: Ruins of Eskibeyazit below Ishak Paşa Sarayi.

Opposite: The buildings of Ishak Paşa Sarayi and some of the ruins of Eskibeyazit, seen from the Urartian citadel.

Mount Ararat dominates the landscape for miles around. 5165 metres (or nearly 17,000 feet) high, you will see its white cone while you are still far away. It is more difficult to climb than might appear at first sight, partly because of the severe and rapid changes of weather which are common on its flanks, and partly because of a very difficult zone of broken lava.

It takes its name from the Prophet Jeremiah's (Jer. 51:4) misspelling of the word Urartu. Whether Noah first touched land after the Flood on Ararat itself, or on some mountain bordering the Mesopotamian plain (which would also have been in the Urartian Empire's territory) remains an open question. Certainly there is ample archaeological evidence that a great Flood did take place in what is today Iraq.

Whatever the truth, the beauty of this volcanic cone, towering over the plains around, cannot fail to impress the traveller. James Morier, passing in 1815, writes that 'I had one of the most extensive and sublime views, perhaps, in the world. The grand outlines of Ararat were on the one side..'' He goes on to mention "The wild animals that inhabit this region are bears, small tygers, lynxes and lions. Perhaps the most dangerous are the serpents, some of which, of a large size, are venomous in the highest degree. When we resided in the vicinity of Ararat, a tale was prevalent that a dragon had got possession of the road which leads between the small and the greater mountain, and had impeded the passage of caravans".

Lions, tygers and dragons are, alas, nowadays in short supply. But the beauty of Ararat remains.

Below: Mount Ararat.

Above: Little Ararat from the slopes
of Mount Ararat, photographed at
sunset, with the shadow of Ararat
clearly visible.

Erzurum has the rough and ready atmosphere of a frontier agricultural town. Indeed it is both. It has been fought over innumerable times; and it lies in the heart of the great pastoral Anatolian plateau. I must confess to a special fondness for this sombre city, two thousand metres above sea level and subject to six month winters of renowned severity; for it was here that my grandfather was born in 1852.

On the ancient site, the city was rebuilt by Theodosius the Great in the second half of the fourth century. The word Erzurum may come from the name given to it by the early Seljuk invaders, Arz-er-Rum, the land of the Romans (i.e. Byzantines). It occupies a strategic position in the centre of the plateau, and it has always been the most important city in the approaches to eastern Anatolia. Each invader in turn has attacked and held the city; most recently the Russians, twice in the 19th century and again in 1916.

The aura of a frontier town is enhanced by stories of wolves until very recently on the university campus in winter. And perhaps the damage done by several severe earthquakes to the older buildings over the centuries enhances it. But here is an atmosphere of industry and skilled craftmanship.

Above: The base of a minaret of the 13th century Seljuk Cifte Minareli Medrese, Erzurum.

Above: Erzurum from a window in the old British Consulate, where the author's grandfather was born in 1852 (Curzon, 1854).

Above: A Seljuk türbe, Erzurum.

CHAPTER IV

LAKE VAN AND THE HAKKARİ

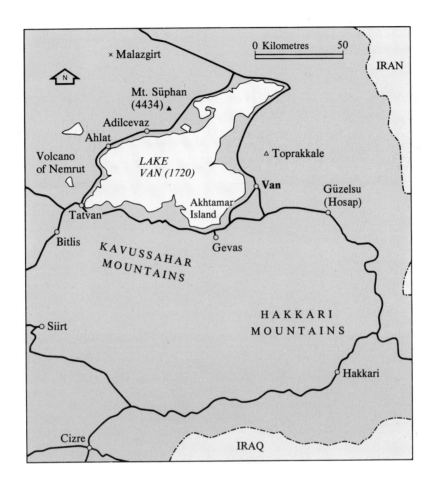

Lake Van is a magical place to visit. For much of the winter the region is bitterly cold; in high summer the scenery is burnt and sere. But come in May or June, when it is spring, and the scenery is breath-taking. The Kavussahar mountains to the south and Süphan Dag (4,434 metres) on the northern shore are snow-capped; their flanks are green with fresh grass; the meadows below are ablaze with carpets of flowers; and the lake itself is a brilliant azure blue.

The lake is high, at 1720 metres or 5600 feet; and large, covering 3,750 square kilometres, six times the size of Lake Geneva.

The water is highly alkaline and therefore somewhat buoyant; after bathing one is left with a delicious silky feeling on the skin. There are few fish, except where rivers bring fresh water to the lake's edge.

Perhaps the best way to appreciate all the moods of this splendid lake is to spend not less than two days driving around its edge. Van and Tatvan make convenient night stopping places. You will view Urartian fortresses and Seljuk tombs; ancient citadels and an extraordinary 10th centruy Armenian church set on a perfect island; a vast eight hundred year old cemetery; the enormous crater of Nemrut Dag, seven kilometres across. All these will be seen in the setting of the mountains, flowers and a lake of unsurpassed beauty.

Opposite: Storm over Lake Van.

The Urartu civilisation flourished in eastern Anatolia for some three centuries, 900-600 BC. Taking advantage of weakness in its better known rival Assyria in the late ninth century BC, the Urartians gradually enlarged their empire. At its height, in the early eighth century BC, it spread from beyond the Caucasus to the northern Syrian plains and even to the Mediterranean. Under King Menua (c 810 - 786 BC) and his son Argistis I (c 786 - 764 BC) it was the most powerful state in western Asia. But the Assyrians revived and the second half of the eighth and all of the seventh centuries BC saw an endless and bloody struggle between the two great rivals. This weakened both empires and allowed the rise of new powers. The Assyrian Empire departed from history in a single day, with the fall of Nineveh in 612 BC; about twenty years later the Medes overthrew Urartu.

The Urartians gave their name to Mount Ararat. In history they are known as skilled metal workers, tremendous builders and ingenious engineers. For over a century the area around Lake Van in particular flowered with towns and fortresses, aqueducts and irrigation canals.

The heart of the Urartian Empire was the citadel of Van. Nearby, at Toprakkale, above and behind Van, lie the remains of the eighth century BC royal palace of an Urartian king.

Opposite: Entrance to the 8th century BC royal palace at Toprakkale, with the typical Urartian ledges for decorative stone facing.

Below: Simple sturdy carts with solid wheels, unchanged over millenia, near Lake Van.

The rock citadel of Van, Van Kalesi, has obvious very strong natural defence characteristics. Shaped like the dorsal fin of a sail fish, it runs west to east away from the lake; it rises out of a very flat lakeside plain, and therefore offers excellent views in all directions.

Its history is appropriately military. It became the capital of the Urartian Empire in the ninth century BC. It withstood the Assyrian onslaught, most notably in 735 BC when the Assyrian King Tiglath-Pileser III besieged the great rock. The Armenians succeeded the Urartians in north-eastern Anatolia, founding their first Kingdom in the 4th century BC. Looking more to Persia than Rome, Van dwindled in importance over the centuries, until it briefly became the capital of a new Armenian state in the seventh century AD.

Persian, Mongol and Turkoman invasions swept over Van. Timur destroyed it in 1387. In 1534 it surrendered to Suleiman the Magnificent, and has been Turkish since, although Kurdish princes have often held actual local power. The expulsion of the Armenians and the Kurdish revolts of this century have continued Van's troubled history.

But today it is a wonderfully evocative place to visit, especially on a spring evening in May or early June when the ghosts of ancient warrior rulers may be heard whispering on the wind. With the snow clad mountains to the south, and gold on the lake's waters, who knows what ancient plans are being discussed.

Below: Sunset over western fortifications of the citadel at Van, the lake behind.

Opposite: Old Van at sunset.

On the south and steepest side of Van Kalesi there are rooms and passages cut through the rock. Along the outside walls and on a suitable buttress are cuneiform inscriptions dating from the eighth to the fifth centuries BC. They were carved more than two thousand five hundred years ago, yet they remain in an excellent state of preservation. They record the martial, religious and architectural exploits of Urartian and then Persian kings. More would survive but for the rage of Timur, who could not decipher what he took to be magical secrets.

Left: Marvellously preserved cuneiform writing on the steep south flank of the citadel at Van.

Opposite: The citadel at Van, with its steep south facing cliff, and the ruins of the old city below.

Over, pages 108-109: The island of Akhtamar in Lake Van with its well-preserved 10th century Armenian church.

The setting for the best preserved of all early Armenian churches is superb. For in the early 10th century A.D. King Gagik I Artzruni made the island of Akhtamar in Lake Van one of the principal seats of his Kingdom. Not much remains of his palace at the summit of the hill on the little island, nor of his monastery. But the Church of the Holy Cross, built between 915 and 921, is wonderfully preserved. The most unusual and interesting feature of the church is the sculptures in projecting relief on its outside walls. Animals and hunters, birds and vines set off stylised Biblical stories. Eve does not look as if she would tempt Adam, and David appears somewhat untrustworthy, but the overall effect is both startling and very pleasing indeed.

Very worthwhile is the walk to the top of the hill. From here you may view the incomparable setting of King Gagik's retreat. And there is no better place in all the Van region than the island for a picnic and a swim.

Opposite: The carvings in relief at Akhtamar are well preserved. The Apostles watch over various Biblical scenes, including Jonah being fed to a whale.

Below: The 10th century church on Akhtamar island, close to.

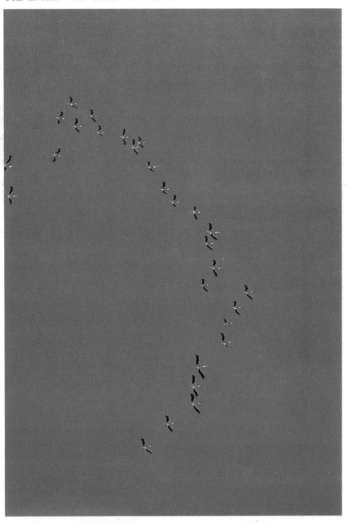

The volcano Nemrut Dag, at the south-west corner of Lake Van, underwent an enormous eruption some 2.8 million years ago. The river which had drained the Van basin was dammed. The result was the creation of Lake Van, which has no outlet. Fine specimens of obsidian, natural black glass created in the heat of volcanos, can be found in the huge crater of Nemrut Dag.

Left: Storks in flight over Lake Van.

Below: The huge volcanic crater of Nemrut Dag, with black obsidian in the foreground.

Opposite: The 14th century Halime Hatun türbe at Gevaş, on the southern shore of Lake Van.

The town of Ahlat has the usual exciting and troubled history of the region. First heard of as an Armenian town of importance, it fell to the Arabs in the seventh century; then to the invading Seljuks in the eleventh century. Two confused centuries of local overlords followed, until the Mongols took it in 1245. More local sovereignty followed until it was seized by Suleiman the Magnificent in 1533. It soon lost its importance, for Ottoman writ did not extend so far east except in name, and the Kurdish emirs of Bitlis became its overlords.

Above: Detail from the Ulu or great türbe at Ahlat, dating from the 13th century.

But one does not go to Ahlat to see the remains of the 16th century walls, citadels or mosques. For the glory of Ahlat is its cemetery. As John Freely has written, this is "a veritable petrified forest of lichen-covered gravestones dating back to Seljuk times, many of them finely carved and adorned with calligraphic and floral designs. This is surely one of the most romantically beautiful graveyards in the world."

Above: The cemetery at Ahlat.

Pages 116-117, over: Mt. Süphan, 4434 metres high, in spring, seen across part of Lake Van.

The Hakkari Mountains of south-eastern Turkey are sparsely inhabited. The population is in the main semi-nomadic, sitting out the long and harsh winter months in their villages; and in summer moving with their flocks to the high pastures.

Above: Shepherd boy in the Hakkari mountains.

Opposite: Shepherds in the high Hakkari mountains, the men with their distinctive felt all-weather protective coats.

The summer campsites are remote and often in fine situations. But the summer is short, and after a few months the Hakkari people must retreat to their villages for the winter.

Above: Across much of Asia nomadic women weave on such ground looms. Colourful sacks are being woven in the centre; to the right is a panel of a black tent.

Left: Women spinning and knitting in a tent.

Opposite: A high camp in the Hakkari for summer grazing.

The far south-eastern corner of Turkey has been an area over the ages not of empires but of fiercely independent village and tribal life. Hoşap castle, some 60 kms from Van on the road into the Hakkari mountains, above the village of Güzelsu, is a reminder of the Power these local chieftains once had. Built first in the 15th century and then completely rebuilt in the mid- 17th century by Sarı Süleiman of the Mahmudi tribe, it commands the neighbouring countryside. The setting high above the river is superb, and the scale of the walls which wander over the nearby hills implies the considerable power of an unusually successful mountain robber baron.

Below: Fortifications and huge cistern at Hoşap.

Opposite: The castle at Hoşap, brooding over the River Engel.

CHAPTER V

THE SOUTH: DİYARBAKIR TO ADANA

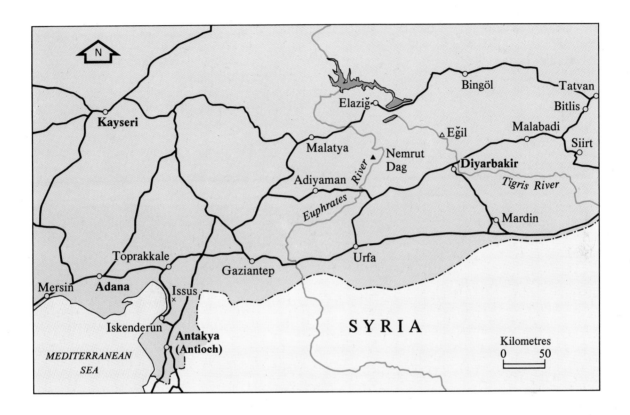

The southern frontier of Turkey is crowded with history. Countless armies have marched this way, and their kings and generals are almost a roll-call of ancient history.

Away from the Mediterranean there is for the most part a hard Asiatic plateau climate; hot and dry in summer, very cold in winter. Spring and autumn are the best times to travel here. The distances are considerable, but the journey is well worthwhile.

Opposite: The graceful bridge over the Batman river at Malabadi, built in 1146.

Cahit Sitki Taranci (1910-56), one of Turkey's leading 20th century poets, was born in Diyarbakir. He is best known for his poem, "My Thirty-Fifth Year"; these are the first and last verses:

Yaş otuzbeş, yolun yarısı eder,
Dante gibi ortasındayız ömrün.
Delikanlı çağımızdaki cevher
Yalvarmak yakarmak nafile bugün,
Gözünün yaşına bakmadan gider.

Neylersin ölüm herkesin başında.
Uyudun uyanamadın olacak,
Kim bilir nerde,, nasıl, kaç yaşında?
Bir namazlık saltanatın olacak,
Taht misali o musalla taşında.

Age: thirty-five and half way to the ending,
Dante-like poised at a lifespan's mid-point.
Despite all your tears, the rule is unbending
Pointless it is now to beg or to plead,
Youth's bright hard substance to nothing is tending

Whatever happens, we'll all find our death here.
Everyone's sleep without waking will come,
In what way, at which age and where is not clear,
Yet Glorious we'll reign for one moment of prayertime
In front of the mosque, as throne: the stone bier.

Below: The house of Cahit Sitki Taranci in Diyarbakir.

Opposite: Carpet shop in a rebuilt medieval caravanserai, Diyarbakir.

The long sombre walls of black basalt give Diyarbakir an air of ancient impregnability. The city, on a bluff high above a bend in the river Tigris, is indeed strategically placed, and has been fought over by innumerable invaders. In the museum you may find relics of its former inhabitants: Hurrians, Mitanni, Assyrians, Medes, Persians, Seljuks, Turkomans and finally Ottomans. The walls were originally Roman; it was an important eastern outpost of the Empire. They were greatly improved by Justinian in the 6th century, who added to the defence towers to make a total of seventy eight along their five and half kilometre length. They were again restored and strengthened in the 12th and 13th centuries by the Seljuks.

Its classical name was Amida. When the city fell to the Arabs in 639 it was occupied by the Beni Bakr tribe, who gave it its present name, Diyarbakir, the place or home of the Bakr. Apart from its magnificent fortifications Diyarbakir is also famous for its produce - especially its melons, fertilised by the rich mud of the Tigris - and for the many mosques in the city.

Opposite: Part of the cloth market in Diyarbakir, with the square minaret of the 11th century Ulu Cami, the very first of the great Seljuk mosques in Anatolia.

Below: The basalt walls of Diyarbakir.

In the 5th century BC when Xenophon and his ten thousand cut their way northwards across the Anatolian Plateau to the Black Sea, they passed through many forests. The combination of millennia of tree-felling and the goat has reduced much of the plateau to an almost treeless landscape. Nevertheless pockets of forest allow the age-old industry of the forester to continue.

Over, pages 132-133: The heads of Zeus and Apollo on Nemrut Dag, the mountains of Commagne behind.

Above: Logs lashed into rafts being transported down the Tigris.

Above: The massive Assyrian fortifications at Eğil, 40 kms north-north-west of Diyarbakir, on the Tigris.

Above: Assyrian tombs at Eğil.

An altogether splendid place, one of the wonders of Turkey, Nemrut Dag is best visited in the late afternoon, to catch the setting sun on the westward facing terrace. When the Seleucid Empire, founded by Seleucus, one of Alexander's generals, collapsed in the first century BC, the smallish Kingdom of Commagne was carved out by Mithradates I. The Kingdom reached its zenith under Antiochus I, 64-32 BC, and for over a century, until it was annexed by Vespasian in 72 AD, Commagne served as a useful buffer between Rome and the ever threatening Parthia to the East. In Roman times it was well-timbered and richly pastured, but today it is treeless and dry.

The sanctuary on top of Nemrut Dag, 2000 metres high, is on a vast scale. There are large platforms on the eastern and western sides of a huge man-made tumulus, under which Antiochus himself may well be buried. The huge carvings of the gods, Zeus and Hercules, Apollo and Antiochus, gaze over the mountains around, frost-damaged but imperious.

Above: The head of Apollo, Nemrut Dag.

Opposite: The head of Zeus, Nemrut Dag.

Above: Eagle's head, Nemrut Dag.

Urfa is a very ancient town, its citadel affording a strategic vantage point over the Syrian plains to the south. It was occupied in the Bronze Age, the second millennium BC, by the Hurrians. Its rich grazing must have been an added attraction for its early settlers. Alexander's veterans settled here in the latter part of the fourth century BC, and renamed the place Edessa, after a town in their homeland Macedonia. It suffered the usual vicissitudes of frontier towns, being besieged and taken by successive invaders. It became famous as a Christian principality for a brief half century, 1098-1144. It was captured early on the First Crusade by Baldwin of Flanders, and became the seat of the Counts of Edessa. Retaken by the Seljuks in 1144 and finally in 1146 from the Crusaders, it fell to Hulagu, the Great Khan of the Mongols, in 1260.

There are many legends which associate Urfa with Abraham, an important figure to Muslims. A favourite concerns King Nimrod. Abraham disapproved of Nimrod's polytheism, and smashed the idols in the temple. Abraham was condemned to death by fire. As the fire was too hot for the executioners to approach, Abraham was catapulted into it. As he landed a miraculous spring appeared, to break his fall. Today the spring is a very holy Muslim shrine, full of carp that no one is allowed to catch.

Edessa was a seat of Christian learning in the Syriac tongue during the late Byzantine rule. Many Greek manuscripts were translated into Syriac, and eventually found their way into Arabic. With the coming of European Renaissance the Arabic was in turn translated, and the classical sources preserved.

Below: The holy carp in Abraham's pool, Urfa.

Opposite: The delightful 13th century Khalil Medresesi, beside Abraham's pool, Urfa.

The castle of Toprakkale dominates the junction of the east-
west Diyarbakir to Adana road, and the route to Antioch
and the south. This has clearly always been an important
crossroad, and countless armies have marched past this
great mound. The castle itself was probably built in the 10th
century. During the 12th century it was successively held by
the Byzantines, Armenians and Crusaders. It was finally
captured and destroyed by the Mamluks in the 13th
century, and was never restored.

Below: The castle of Toprakkale.

The probable site of the battle of Issus (the exact location is still disputed by scholars) is today mostly built over. For just south of the oil port of Dörtyol a large industrial complex has grown up in recent years. The scene depicted in this lithograph is as it was in the mid-19th century. But it is impossible to drive down this coast, past all those modern buildings, without thinking of the battle which changed the face of the ancient world in 333 BC, when the greatly outnumbered army of Alexander defeated the massed might of the greatest Empire the world had seen.

Below: The site of the battle of Issus
(W.H.Bartlett, 1836).

Above: Alexander the Great (mosaic from Pompeii, now in Museo Nazionale, Naples).

Opposite: Darius of Persia in his chariot (mosaic from Pompeii, now in Museo Nazionale, Naples).

The first great world empire was that of the Persians; they ruled from the Aegean to the Hindu Kush. In 585 BC they had entered Anatolia, and in 546 BC they defeated Croesus of Lydia. Thereafter for two hundred years they ruled the Anatolian Peninsula, twice using it as the starting point for unsuccessful expeditions against Greece (in 490 and 480 BC).

Athens and Sparta dissipated their strength in endless wars, and this allowed Macedonia to rise to prominence under the energetic leadership of Philip (382-336 BC). His son Alexander (356-323 BC) secured Greece with a series of rapid masterstrokes in 335 and then he set out for Asia.

Darius III, the Great King of Persia, gathered his armies together to meet this Macedonian menace. In November 333 BC the two armies met on the narrow plain of Issus, by the Mediterranean shore. The Persian army greatly outnumbered the Macedonians, but was hampered by lack of space. The shock of Alexander's angled cavalry charge shattered the Persian nerve, and Darius fled. Some contemporary stories of the battle tell of a face to face encounter between Alexander and Darius, and this mosaic captures the turning point of the battle, as Darius' chariot is turned from the fray.

When Alexander the Great died at the age of 33 in 323 BC, his generals divided up his world empire between them. Seleucus took Babylonia, and in 301 BC defeated the One-Eyed Antigonus, thereby gaining Syria and much of what is Turkey today as well. He thereupon moved his capital from the Tigris to the Mediterranean, founding Seleucia on the coast and Antioch thirty kilometres inland within a month of each other in 300 BC. His son moved the capital of the empire from the former to Antioch, and for two centuries Antioch remained the centre of the Seleucid Empire. This empire collapsed in 83 BC, and it was soon annexed to the Roman Empire. In 64 BC Pompey made Antioch capital of the Roman province of Syria. It soon became one of the leading cities of the age, with a population which may have approached half a million; a huge figure for those days, surpassed only by Alexandria and Rome itself.

Below: The Church of St. Peter, who is said to have preached here at Antakya, the ancient Antioch.

Alas, this once great city has been beset by catastrophe, caused both by man and by nature. For the site is both difficult to defend and prone to earthquake. In the 3rd century it was twice sacked by the Sassanians from Persia, on the second occasion being also devastated by fire; in 540 the Persians again destroyed the city; they occupied it in 611; the Byzantines recaptured it in 628; the Arabs routed the Byzantines in 638 and took the city, occupying it until 969, when the Byzantines recaptured it yet again; in 1084 it was captured by the Seljuks; in 1098 the Crusaders took it after a long and bloody siege, and for one hundred and seventy years it was the capital of a Frankish principality. In 1268 the city was utterly destroyed by the Mamluks. The city never recovered, and over the centuries it dwindled until in the 19th century it was little more than a remote village, surrounded by the remnants of vast and once magnificent fortifications. Today it has recovered a certain provincial prosperity.

Above: An artist's impression of the walls of Antioch as seen in the mid 19th century. (W.H. Bartlett, 1836).

Above: Mosaic of Orpheus playing to the beasts, late 3rd century AD, (Antakya museum).

Antakya (or Antioch as it was) has been ravaged by so many catastrophes, both man-inspired and natural, that little remains to be seen of the ancient city in situ. Fortunately much of what does remain has been rescued and is preserved in what is one of the most interesting smaller museums in Turkey. Here on the bank of the Orontes is a superb collection of Roman mosaics, which hint at the importance of this city in classical times.

Opposite: Courtyard of the museum at Antakya, the ancient Antioch.

On the west bank of the Ceyhan River, within easy driving distance from Adana, is the formidable castle of Yilankale, the castle of the snake. In legend this is reputed to have been the home of the King of the Snakes. In fact it was probably built in the 12th century by King Leo II of Lesser Armenia. Subsequently it was occupied by the Crusaders. The site, high on an outcrop above a great bend in the river, is magnificent. From its highest point you may view the vast Cilician plain, a cradle of early civilisation, with over 150 ancient Neolithic and Chalcolithic sites dotted about. The mounds or tepes, the result of millennia of building and living, are clearly visible.

Below: The Ceyhan River with castle of Yilankale and surrounding hills.

Opposite: View from the citadel of Yilankale, with the Ceyhan river and plain below.

Adana stands in the middle of the Cilician Plain, for
thousands of years an area of rich agriculture. Moreover it is
on the main route to the Cilician Gates, one of the few
routes through the forbidding Taurus Mountains to the
Anatolian Plateau behind. Thus strategically situated, it is
not surprising that it has been overrun by an endless
succession of invaders. Although not the earliest, the first
recorded are the Hittites in the 14th century BC. Assyrians,
Persians, Seleucids, Romans, Arabs, Seljuks, Armenians,
Crusaders, Mamelukes, Ottomans and in this century even
briefly the French have ruled Adana. Today it is Turkey's
fourth city, a bustling thriving centre of activity.

Below: Tobacco farmers waiting to
sell their crop, Antakya.

Opposite: The Ulu Cami or Great
Mosque at Adana, built in 1507.

CHAPTER VI

THE SOUTH COAST

The southern shore of Turkey is one of long sandy beaches and rocky headlands. The interior is cut off by the massive bulk of the Taurus Mountains, a formidable barrier which is not easily crossed. Behind are the highlands of the Anatolian Plateau, the birthplace of early civilisations.

Opposite: The Yivli Minare or Fluted Minaret, a 13th century Seljuk minaret, Antalya.

Antalya is strategically located in a magnificent setting at the head of the large gulf which bears its name. Across the bay the mountains of Lycia rise to 10,000 feet, with the peaks of Mount Solymnos and Mount Climax often snow-covered. Founded relatively late by the King of Pergamum in the mid-second century BC, it passed to Rome shortly afterwards in 133 BC.

The Romans found it useful both as a centre for trade and as a base for suppressing the pirates who operated from the Lycian coasts to the west and the Cilician coasts to the east. During the early Crusades Antalya was often the port of embarkation for the Latin armies seeking to avoid the difficult land march. The Seljuks took it from the Byzantines in 1207, and there are some fine remains from their century of rule. Today Antalya is well placed both for the magnificent beaches to the east and as a base for archaeological excursions.

Opposite: The Castle of Anamur is the largest of all the medieval strongholds on the Mediterranean coast of Turkey. After many vicissitudes the castle was restored by the Ottomans in 1840 and was in use for the rest of the 19th century.

Below: The harbour, Antalya.

In the 11th century many Armenians had been forced by successive Seljuk invasions to leave north-east Anatolia to seek sanctuary under Byzantine rule along the shores of the Mediterranean. During the first half of the 12th century they succeeded in carving out an Armenian Kingdom in Cilicia, with effective independence from Byzantium. They built a number of castles along the coast, ruling the area for nearly three hundred years. They maintained their independence by adroit marriage alliances with the not too distant Crusader Kingdoms. But the 14th century was a period of turmoil in south-eastern Anatolia, with the onslaught of the Mongols proving too much for many of the minor kingdoms of the time. It was a time of confusion and chaos. In 1375 the last Armenian stronghold fell.

Below and opposite: The Kizkalesi, or Maiden's Castle, was built in the mid-12th century. This castle was once connected to the castle on the beach.

On the road from Silifke to Konya, some 20 kilometres
north of Mut, lies Alahan. The early centuries of Byzantine
rule, and especially the 5th and 6th centuries, saw the
building of many churches throughout Asia Minor. One of
the finest and most interesting of these church sites is at
Alahan, where there are ruins of a monastery, two churches
and a baptistry. The oldest of these dates back to about 450
AD. The main 5th century church is known as the Church
of the Four Evangelists; it has fine arches and interesting
relief carvings over the entrance. The position is spectacular,
for the complex is perched on a platform overlooking the
Göksu Gorge.

Below: 5th century Christian ruins,
Alahan.

Opposite: The Church of the Four
Evangelists, Alahan.

Alanya was known in antiquity as Coracesium, and was of minor importance, serving mainly as a base for the pirates who plagued the coasts of southern Turkey. Pompey changed all this in 67 BC. A lightning three month campaign against the pirates culminated in a final sea battle off Coracesium. Pompey's victory was total; piracy was ended. And Coracesium disappeared from history for more than a thousand years, becoming no more than a minor trading port under the Romans, the Byzantines and the Armenians. Its main trade was the export of Anatolian timber to Egypt.

The Seljuks took it in 1221 (under their great Sultan, Keykûbad I, 1219-34) and renamed it the 'city of Alâ', Alâiye. The Sultan constructed the magnificent fortifications which may be seen hardly altered today. Alâiye now became an impregnable fortress, cultural centre and trading entrepot.

With the collapse of the Seljuk hegemony at the end of the 13th century, Alâiye fell to the independent Karamanlis emirs. When Ibn Battuta, the great Arab traveller, arrived in 1333, he found it a thriving trading town. It fell to the Ottomans in 1471, but once they captured Cyprus, a hundred years later, its strategic importance was gone and serious decline began. An early 19th century traveller found an unimportant town and miserable houses. The present prosperity is the result of recent developments.

Above all, the superb fortifications and buildings of the Aleppo architect of Sultan Keykûbad have remained for three quarters of a millennium.

Below and Opposite: The cliffs of Alanya.

Above and below: The Kizil Kule or Red Tower, the key to the defences of Alanya, built in 1226.

Opposite: The walls and gardens of Alanya.

Aspendus is mentioned in the 8th century BC in Hittite inscriptions. But it is as the site of the Athenian General Cimon's brilliant defeat of the Persians both at sea and on land in a single day that Aspendus first made its mark in history.

The early attempts of the Persians to subjugate Greece, by Darius in 490 BC and by Xerxes ten years later, ended in utter defeat. Xerxes wished to try again, and by 468 BC had assembled a large army and fleet at Aspendus. Cimon of Athens decided on a preemptive raid. A fiercely contested sea battle on the River Eurymedon, beneath the walls of Aspendus, ended in victory for Cimon. Dressing his men in captured Persian uniforms, and sailing in captured Persian ships at dusk, he hoodwinked the Persian guards and infiltrated the enemy camp. A land victory was quickly and decisively won.

Under Rome Aspendus prospered. In the second century AD, in the reign of Marcus Aurelius, the architect Zeno constructed the superb and monumental theatre of Aspendus. Built to seat 20,000 in comfort, on a recent occasion it is said to have held double that number.

Termessus, set high in the mountains behind Antalya, should be visited in spring, when wild flowers lend extra beauty to an already magical site. The ancient city stands at 1050 metres on a saddle between the old Mount Solymus and another mountain. The inhabitants were warlike and independent, and referred to themselves as Solymian; there were no Greek settlers. Alexander skirmished with the Termessians in 333 BC, but found the city too well protected to be worth attacking. And later in a treaty with Rome, they were treated as near equals, "friends and allies", with the right "to be ruled by their own laws".

The site is extremely beautiful, with scattered sarcophagi and tombs overgrown with trees and flowers; and the view from the theatre, over the precipice of Mount Solymus, is breathtaking.

Below: The theatre of Zeno at Aspendus.

Opposite and over, pages 164-165: the theatre at Termessus.

Çatal Hüyük is one of the most important archaeological sites in all Turkey. James Mellaart organised the excavations here which established that the site dated back to the 7th millennia BC, and these led to huge strides in our knowledge of Neolithic and Bronze Age Cultures in Anatolia. The site itself is mere mud walls impregnated with shards of pottery; for a glimpse of the sophisticated level of culture attained so early you must visit the Hittite Museum in Ankara. When visiting the site, it is important to remember that this area would have been heavily wooded in ancient times.

The Göksu Gorge is one of the few ways through the Taurus Mountains, and leads from the Mediterranean to the highlands of the Anatolian Plateau. The way is spectacular, with high cliffs and spires of rock menacing the road.

Many ancient and medieval generals and travellers have passed this way. Perhaps the most unfortunate was the Emperor Frederick Barbarossa, who in June 1190 was drowned attempting to ford the river as he led his army on the Third Crusade. This was certainly an inauspicious beginning to a disastrous crusade. Today the traveller faces no such risks. But he may admire the rugged grandeur of this route to the north.

Above: The Göksu Gorge.

Above: The site of Çatal Hüyük.

Above: Water buffalo enjoying a mud pool.

Konya is a green oasis in what during summer is a very hot plateau steppe. With water in abundance, this was a natural site for neolithic settlement. The name has remained essentially unchanged for 4000 years; the Hittites called it Kuwanna, the Phrygians Kowania, the Greeks Ikonian, the Romans and Byzantines Iconium, the Saracens Kûniye, and now the Turks call it Konya.

The main interest of Konya is twofold. First, it has the finest Seljuk buildings in Turkey. In the early 12th century it became the capital of the Seljuks of Rum, and for the next two hundred years there was much architectural and artistic activity. Second, it was the birthplace and home of the founder of the Mevlevi order of the whirling dervishes, Mevlâna Celâleddin Rumî, who died in 1273. Every December there is a Festival of Mevlâna in Konya, when visitors have an opportunity to see the whirling Mevlâna dance.

Opposite: Detail of a corner in the Karatay Medrese at Konya, built 1251-2. The inverted Turkish triangles transfer the weight of the round dome to the corners of the building.

Below: The Mevlâna Museum, Konya, which contains the tomb of the founder of the Mevlevi order.

CHAPTER VII

THE SOUTH-WEST : ANTALYA TO İZMİR

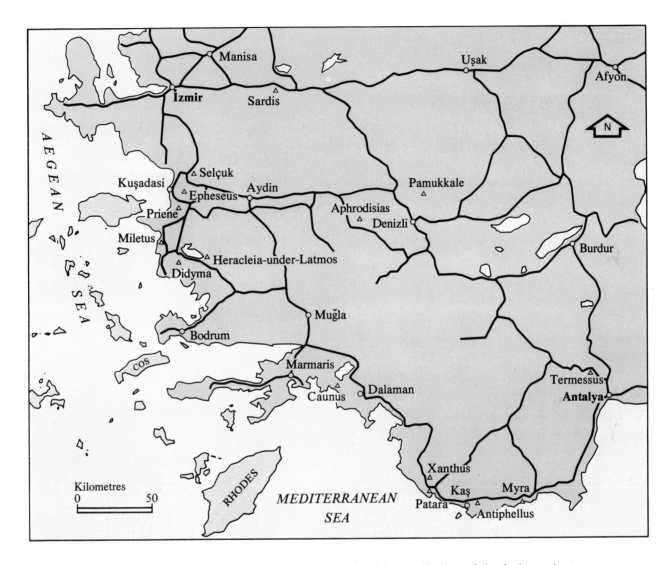

The area between Antalya and Izmir comprises the richest collection of classical remains to be found anywhere. The coastline is also one of outstanding beauty. Although parts are fast being developed for tourism, there are many peaceful out-of-the way places for the traveller to explore.

This chapter includes ancient Lycia, Caria, Ionia and parts of Lydia. In a guide written eighteen centuries ago Pausanias wrote: "Ionia enjoys the finest of climates and its sanctuaries are unmatched in the world". He might as well have been writing about the whole of this area.

Opposite: Poppies in profusion, south-west Turkey.

Xanthus was the most important of all Lycian cities, and was often the capital of the region. It is also one of the most ancient cities, dating from at least the eighth century BC.

Its fame however rests on the heroic nature of its citizens. Twice they resisted invasion literally to the last inhabitant. The first time was against the advance of the army of Cyrus the Great of Persia in the sixth century BC. The second time was five hundred years later, in 42 BC, resisting the Romans under Brutus. Herodotus records the first event thus:

> "When Harpagus advanced into the plain of the Xanthus, they met him in battle, though greatly outnumbered, and fought with much gallantry; at length, however, they were defeated and forced to retire within their walls, whereupon they collected their women, children, slaves and other property and shut them up in the citadel of the city, set fire to the place and burned it to the ground. Then having sworn to do or die, they marched out to meet the enemy and were killed to a man."

Myra must have been an important town by the fifth century BC. But in most respects history passed it by. The result was prosperous obscurity.

Myra's fame rests on its 7th century AD bishop, St. Nicholas. Patron saint of virgins and children, sailors and scholars, he later became the patron saint of both Greece and Russia. His fame as a gift bringer derives from the time when he heard of a bankrupt merchant who could find no dowry for his three daughters. Unseen he threw three bags of gold into the merchant's house. From this grew the legend of secret present giving and his eventual transformation into Santa Claus.

On the eastern shore of Lycia, there is an ever-burning natural gas seepage, unimpressive by day, but visible for miles by night. This is the origin of the Greek myth of the Chimaera, the fire-breathing monster which was thought to dwell in Lycia. Homer described it in the Iliad: "Chimaera ..... breathed dread fierceness of blazing fire".

Left: The Obelisk at Xanthus, inscribed on all four sides in so far untranslated Lycian.

Above: Lycian rock tombs near Caunus.

Above: Rock tombs near Myra.

Above: The fire of the Chimaera by day.

In ancient times Patara was a flourishing port, serving Xanthus in particular. Alexander, Hannibal and St. Paul were amongst those who passed through. It was famed for its Oracle of Apollo, which at one time rivalled that of Delphi. St. Nicholas (Santa Claus) of Myra was born here.

Today the famous harbour is no more. In common with so many ancient Mediterranean harbours, the harbour which brought Patara wealth and fame has silted up. Deposits carried down by the river Xanthus have cut it off from the sea. The site is deserted and today the drifting sand dunes and the sea birds possess the theatre. A good place for a quiet picnic.

One of the highlights of any tour of the Lycian coast (roughly Dalaman to Antalya), whether by land or sea, must be the splendid harbour setting of Kaş. The road runs steeply down through the town to the water's edge; the setting, with a great vertical cliff dominating behind, and the coves and inlets of the peninsula of Kaş, is striking indeed. This is definitely a place for a night's stop.

Antiphellus, the ancient city, began life as a humble port for Phellus. But as commercial intearests became more important in Hellenistic times, so Antiphellus grew in importance and Phellus declined. Today only the theatre, set superbly for sea views, reminds us of the bustle of the ancient port.

Below: The theatre at Antiphellus.

Opposite: The sand-filled theatre at Patara.

Marmaris is today an important yachting centre. It is ideally set at the end of a long fiord, where Nelson sheltered his fleet in 1798. The town was largely destroyed by an earthquake in 1958, and is now being built anew.

Above: The harbour at Marmaris.

Above: Yacht in a hidden bay West of Marmaris.

Bodrum is ancient Halicarnassus. If the approach is by land, the road which winds through the foothills of Kaplan Dagi (the Tiger's mountain), presents the traveller with a superb approach to the city; if by sea, the first view will be of the castle and the port.

Ancient Halicarnassus was the site of one of the seven wonders of the world, the vast mausoleum of the fourth century BC Persian Satrap or governor Mausolus. Indeed this was the period of the city's greatest prosperity, for Mausolus was the virtually independent ruler of Caria, and under his powerful rule Halicarnassus became rich. The mausoleum built by his sister-wife for Mausolus was the largest by far of the Greek world, and also one of the most beautiful.

Halicarnassus' great days ended with the siege by Alexander the Great, when much of the city was destroyed. It became a quiet backwater, a fishing and sponge port, harried by pirates through the centuries. When Timur temporarily loosened the Ottoman hold on Anatolia, the Knights of St. John of Rhodes took the town in 1402 and shortly afterwards began building the Castle of St. Peter, which today dominates the harbour. They found the Mausoleum in ruins, and they pillaged the stones and pillars for the castle. It eventually fell in 1522 to Suleiman the Magnificent, and the Knights retired to Malta.

But the greatest glory of Halicarnassus is its fame as the birthplace of the world's first historian. Herodotus was born here about 485 BC. His "Histories" of the Persian Wars are a magnificent mine of information, and are written with such a light touch that they are a joy to read.

Today Bodrum has become the yachting centre of South-Western Turkey. However commercialized it may become, both its beauty and its place in history are assured.

Above: The Castle at Bodrum (Luigi Mayer, 1804).

Above: Part of Bodrum from the harbour.

Above: The Castle at Bodrum.

Above: A Lycian farmer.

Above: High in the Lycian mountains a farmer travels in a time-honoured way.

Heracleia-under-Latmos is at the eastern end of what in antiquity was a gulf leading to the sea, but which is today a fresh-water lake. With the mountain of Latmos rising behind, and with the serene and placid lake before, it is not difficult to believe in the legend of Heracleia. For it was on the slopes of Mount Latmos that the young shepherd Endymion was sleeping when the moon goddess Selere fell deeply in love with him. Zeus agreed that Endymion should sleep forever, retaining perpetual youth, without ageing; Selere lay with him in his sleep and over time bore him fifty daughters.

The site is well worth visiting. The curious tombs cut into the headland above the water level lend an unusual air to a splendid setting.

Above: Necropolis at the water's edge at Heracleia.

Above: Island fortifications at Heracleia.

Priene was never of the same order of importance as its neighbours Miletus or Ephesus. Two things distinguish it. First, its splendid site on the slopes of Mount Mycale, overlooking the plain of the Meander River. And second, that on its territory was the main meeting place and sanctuary of the Ionian cities; this site was called the Panionium.

Priene was originally further inland, but had to move in the 4th century BC to stay near the sea, as the Meander carried silt into the shallow bay. The view across to Miletus must have been spectacular when the whole of what is today a swampy plain was a glittering bay, full of ancient merchantmen. The most important monument in Priene was the Temple of Athena, and its impressive remains may be seen today; Alexander helped to finance its building.

When visiting Priene and Miletus or indeed Epheseus, it is important to remember that the coastline has altered radically over the centuries. This change results mainly from the silting up of the estuaries with the alluvial discharge of the rivers. Without this knowledge a site such as Miletus would seem inexplicably placed, high and dry in the middle of nowhere. The map on this page indicates where the coastline would have been in classical times.

Left: Flowers in the wall at Priene.

Opposite: Columns in the Temple of Athena at Priene. The plain below was a bay on the Aegean in classical times.

Today the massive remains of the theatre at Miletus seem to be inappropriately stranded. However it was once at the water's edge, on a peninsula jutting into the Aegean. (See map on page 182.) Over the centuries the silt of the Meander river has moved the shoreline some kilometres to the west, leaving Miletus as you see it today.

Although less famous than Epheseus, Miletus was the greatest of all the Ionian ancient cities. Its contribution to civilisation was enormous. Originally it may have been a Cretan port; in the 10th century BC the Ionian Greeks arrived, and Miletus grew to become the most important port and trade centre on the Aegean Coast. During the next three centuries the Milesians were reputed to have founded some ninety colonies in the Mediterranean and the Black Sea.

Alas for all its greatness, it sided against the Persians in the Ionian Revolt which broke out in 499 BC, and after a great sea battle on what is now dry land near the city walls, Miletus fell and was sacked. Miletus remained important through Hellenistic and Roman times, but never regained her predominant position on the coast. Over the following centuries, as the harbour continued to silt up, Miletus declined further, until by the time the Ottomans arrived in the 15th century there was no more than a tiny village left. And this was destroyed by an earthquake in 1955. The huge theatre remains the single reminder of a greatness of nearly three thousand years ago.

Opposite: The huge theatre building at Miletus, looking across what once was a bay and a harbour.

Below: Bases of columns, Miletus.

Didyma was never a town in ancient times, but rather an isolated but very important temple. It served the great ancient city of Miletus near by and was connected to it for the 15 kilometres by a sacred way, lined with statues which may now be seen in the British Museum.

This was the site of one of the most important of all oracles of antiquity, rivalling that of Apollo at Delphi. By the 7th century BC it was famous and housed a great treasure, augmented by rich gifts from Croesus of Sardis in Lydia. Alas, the Persians in 494 BC included Didyma in the punishment of Miletus for its part in the Ionian Revolt, and the shrine was destroyed and the treasure confiscated. The oracle remained in operation, however, and in 333 BC it foretold Alexander's eventual triumph over the Persian Empire. Around 300 BC Seleucus began construction of the immense 120 column temple we find today. Work continued for five centuries and was never finally completed.
With the coming of Christianity the oracle was no longer needed. There remains in Didyma one of the most impressive temples in all the world, a masterpiece which cannot fail to impress.

Opposite: Columns of the Temple of Apollo at Didyma.

Below: Detail of a column's base, Didyma.

Ephesus has always had a religious flavour to it. When the first Hellenic settlement was made by the Ionians in about 1000 BC, the site was already an old one. Native Lydians and Carians worshipped at an ancient shrine of Cybele, the Anatolian fertility or mother goddess. The Ionians used the same shrine and merely changed the name to that of the Greek fertility goddess, Artemis. A millennium later Ephesus was the centre in Asia Minor of early Christianity, and when Saint Paul arrived in 53 AD he found a small group of Christians already established. Tradition has it that Saint John and Mary the mother of Jesus came shortly afterwards.

As at Miletus, it is important to know where the ancient coastline ran. For Ephesus was first and foremost an important port, to which traders and pilgrims flocked. When Croesus of Lydia captured Ephesus in 550 BC the Cayster River was already silting up the harbour, so he moved the city seawards. When the Persians destroyed the rival trading centre Miletus in 494 BC for its part in the Ionian Rebellion, Ephesus was the main beneficiary.

Ephesus eventually became the capital of the Roman province of Asia, and then began her period of greatest prosperity. The population may have numbered 250,000, a huge figure for those days, and the city became the principal commercial and banking centre of Asia Minor. A major attraction to ancient travellers and pilgrims was the temple of Artemis, which was four times greater in area than the Parthenon in Athens. It had no less than 127 massive columns each of 20 metres height, and was accounted one of the seven wonders of the world. Alas, its ruins are half-buried in silt. But there is much to study here, from the theatre where Saint Paul preached to 24,000, to the delicate Temple of Hadrian and the splendidly restored Library of Celsus.

The upheavals of later history and the total silting up of the harbour led to its eventual abandonment in medieval times.

Below: Ephesus as seen in the 19th century (Allom and Walsh, 1838).

Opposite: Detail from the Temple of Hadrian, Ephesus.

Above: An impromptu dance by
Turkish students in the huge theatre
at Ephesus.

Opposite: Looking down to the
Library of Celsus, one of the best
preserved library buildings of
antiquity (2nd century AD).

Until a few years ago Kuşadasi was a small fishing port.
Now the caravanserai has been refurbished as a hotel and
the castle as a restaurant and nightclub. The erstwhile village
is today a fast growing tourist centre. As elsewhere along
this coast, the fish restaurants are excellent.

Below: The yacht basin at Kuşadasi.

Opposite: The town and harbour of
Kuşadasi.

Izmir, ancient Smyrna, is the only ancient Ionian city to have survived the vicissitudes of history. It has been helpful that no river threatens to silt up its marvellous natural harbour.

This is an ancient site which has probably been inhabited since the third millennium BC. Homer may have come from Smyrna. It was prosperous by the 7th century BC, but was destroyed by the Lydian King of Sardis around 600 BC. Alexander helped to reconstruct the city almost three hundred years later, and during Hellenistic and Roman times it was again prosperous. Earthquakes and man-made catastrophes (Timur duly destroyed the city and massacred its inhabitants in 1402) meant that the city had to recover again and again, but by 1415 it was in Ottoman hands. Under the Ottomans the natural advantages of Smyrna made it one of the most important commercial cities of their empire. In 1922 a great fire destroyed much of the city. Today Izmir is a thriving modern city, with little visible from its adventurous past.

Above: The harbour of Izmir, ancient Smyrna (Allom and Walsh, 1838).

Opposite: Pottery for sale, south-west Turkey.

Although the ruins of Aphrodisias are among the most impressive classical remains in Turkey, not a great deal is yet known about its pre-Roman history. The site was inhabited from at least the third millennium BC, with the ancient name of Nino, which equates to Cybele, the fertility or mother goddess. Under the Romans the site became sacred to Aphrodite, and a magnificent temple was built in her honour.

The town was prosperous, not least because of her export of fine marble statues to Italy, Greece and elsewhere. As John Freely has written, "it is now apparent that Aphrodisias was the Florence of the Graeco-Roman world, not only adorning its own city with the work of its native sculptors, but shipping their masterpieces to other places around the Mediterranean".

Perhaps the most splendid remains are those of the stadium, about five hundred metres from the Temple of Aphrodite. This is as well-preserved a stadium as exists from classical times, and with the shade of the olive trees and the colour of the flowers in spring it is a magnificent spectacle to contemplate, with its seating for 25,000 spectators; one can almost hear the noise of the races and games.

Cast hither and thither on the waves of numerous invaders, Aphrodisias shrank from the seat of a bishopric in the 5th century AD to a remote village by the 15th, when the Ottomans arrived.

Preceding pages 196-197: The Stadium at Aphrodisias.

Below and opposite: The Temple of Aphrodite, as seen by Charles Fellows in the mid - 19th century, and today.

Opposite: Patterns of beauty at Pamukkale.

Right and below: Natural thermal springs at a hotel and nearby, Pamukkale.

Pamukkale, 'the cotton castle', is well named. For the lime-bearing thermal springs which flow from the slopes of the hill have over millennia created an extraordinary succession of basins and pools and cliffs, all glistening white. Several Roman emperors came to bathe in these thermal pools and to view this unusual site.

This was ancient Hierapolis, the Holy City, founded in the second century BC and bequeathed to Rome in 133 BC by the last King of Pergamum. All the ruins are Roman. But it is not for the archaeology that you should visit Pamukkale, but rather for a unique manifestation of nature at work.

Above: The precipitous summit of the Acropolis at Sardis.

For nearly 150 years, from the 7th to the mid 6th century BC, Sardis, the capital of Lydia, was the world's richest city. In part this wealth was based on gold washed down by the Pactolus river; sheepskins were spread in the shallows overnight and gold dust collected in the wool. This may have been the origin of the story of the golden fleece.

In Sardis coins were first invented. Early Lydian coins were of electrum, an alloy of gold and silver. The proportions varied, however, and this led to a loss of public confidence. Perhaps for this reason Croesus made the first pure gold and pure silver coins. The new invention spread quickly throughout the whole ancient world.

Croesus was the last and most famous of all Lydian kings, and ruled most of the Anatolian peninsula with a benevolent hand. But in 546 BC he mistook Delphi's oracle which had told him that if he attacked Persia he would bring down a great empire; he attacked, was defeated by Cyrus, and duly brought down his own empire.

Sardis remained important, however, as the residence of a Persian satrap and as the terminus of the Royal Road from Susa. Destroyed by a great earthquake in 17 AD, it was rebuilt by Tiberius. Later it was the seat of an important Christian bishopric. But it was utterly destroyed by Timur in 1401, and literally ceased to exist. 20th century archaeologists had to dig down many feet to unearth the ruins we see today.

Above: The Acropolis at Sardis.

Opposite: Among the columns of the Temple of Artemis at Sardis.

CHAPTER VIII

THE NORTH-WEST : İZMİR TO İZNİK

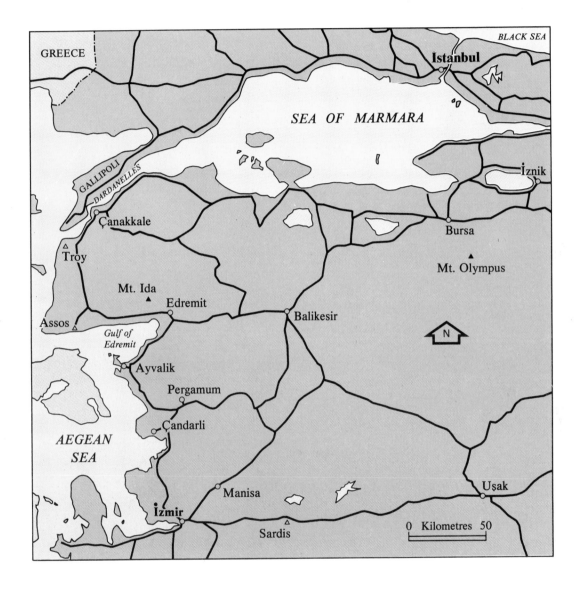

The area between Izmir and Iznik encompasses the ancient provinces of Aeolis, Troas and part of Bithynia. The Aeolians were too busy tending their rich farmlands to make much of a mark on history. Conversely Troas occupied the strategic entrance to the Dardanelles, and through Troy figured prominetly in ancient history.

The drive northwards up the coast is one of surpassing beauty. With the exception of Pergamum there are few magnets to draw the tour buses. Along this coast there are many hidden by-ways which will reward the patient traveller who is in no hurry.

As you turn the corner at Çanakkale and head eastwards towards Bursa and Iznik, the country changes to rolling fields and becomes less maritime. At Bursa you enter the heartland of the Ottoman dynasty.

Opposite: The theatre at Pergamum.

In the first thousand years of its history Pergamum was a
provincial backwater of no particular importance.
Xenophon served here for a year in 400 BC as one of the
Spartan governors, installed by the Persians.

In 281 BC Pergamum fortuitously appeared on the stage of
history. In the decades after the death of Alexander the
Great in 323 BC bitter wars spread over much of Asia as his
generals battled to establish separate empires. Lysimachus
won much of western Anatolia and entrusted the huge
fortune of 9000 talents which he had won in his campaigns
to the citadel of Pergamum for safe-keeping. He appointed
the eunuch Philetairus as his steward of the Treasure. But
when Seleucus invaded Asia Minor in 281 BC Philetairus
turned against his master, siding with the invader.
Lysimachus was defeated and Philetairus confirmed in his
control of Pergamum and the treasure.

By careful but generous gifts to neighbouring cities,
Philetairus and his successors reinforced their position, until
before long Pergamum dominated the whole region. They
also built marvellous palaces, temples and public buildings,
so that at its height in the third and second centuries BC
Pergamum's brilliant culture could be compared with those
of Athens or Alexandria.

Opposite: Restoration work in
progress at Pergamum.

Below: The citadel of Pergamum
(Allom and Walsh, 1838).

Two Kings, Attalus I (241-200 BC) and Eumenes II (200-159 BC), ruled between them for some eighty years. During this period Pergamum first defeated the marauding Gauls in 230 BC in a great battle near the city, thereby removing a dire threat to all of Asia Minor; second, allied itself with Rome, an event with profound effects for Asia Minor; and third, established its hegemony over most of Asia Minor. The fruits of alliance with Rome included much of this last after the battle of Magnesia in 190 BC, when Rome defeated the Syrian Antigonus IV and gave many of the Seleucid possessions in western Anatolia to Pergamum.

The last Attalid King of Pergamum was a mad recluse. He died in 133 BC and willed his city and empire to Rome. It became the core of the Roman province of Asia, but its great days were over, and henceforth it was merely one of many cities, albeit still a prosperous one. Under the Empire it could not rival the importance of Ephesus or Smyrna. Galen the healer was a Pergamene and practised here in the 2nd century AD. The Arabs, returning from their unsuccessful campaign against Constantinople in the 8th century, plundered the city. And so this briefly great cultured and political centre faded from history.

Above: The Basilica or Red Courtyard (Allom and Walsh, 1838).

Opposite: The Basilica still dominates the modern town.

It is difficult to be precise, but there is no doubt that the fish stock of the Mediterranean in general and the Aegean in particular has declined drastically over the past two thousand years. In Roman times the sea was teeming with fish, as mosaics of the period and contemporary historians testify. Today the great fishing fleets of old are shrunk to a few small boats. The fish are as good as ever to eat. But as any scuba diver will testify, there are not very many to be seen.

Above: Looking up to the surface of the Aegean waters.

Opposite: Preparing for a night's fishing.

One of the joys of motoring through Anatolia is the delight of the roadside teahouse. Often in the most picturesque positions and covered with vines, the proprietor is a fount of local knowledge, gossip and hospitality. Teahouses abound from the Bosphorus to the subcontinent and China, all across Asia. But somehow the best Anatolian teahouses are the best of all.

Above: Teahouse proprietor, in the foothills of Mt.Ida.

Opposite: Roadside teahouse near Edremit.

The northern coast of the Gulf of Edremit is one of the most beautiful in all Turkey. There are few archaeological sites between Assos and Pergamum to the south, for the ancient towns have disappeared over the centuries under the building of continuous occupation. For example Edremit itself stands on the site of ancient Adranyttium, but there is not a trace of the latter to be found. It was along this coast that Achilles carried out his raids in the ninth year of the Trojan War. Today there is peace and beauty to be found in abundance along this coastline.

Opposite: Fishing in the Gulf of Edremit.

Over, page 216: Spring in Troas.

Over, page 217: Farmer of Troas.

Below: Village scene on north shore of Gulf of Edremit.

Today ancient Assos is very much in ruins, apart from five columns recently re-erected; and a section of the ancient walls, once among the most impressive in Asia Minor, having been three kilometres in length. The columns are on the highest level of the Acropolis, and are part of the ruins of the 6th century BC Temple of Athena. This is the only archaic Doric temple which has survived in Asia Minor.

Assos was founded three thousand years ago by settlers from the island of Lesbos, opposite the mainland. It was soon a town of commercial importance, both as a transit port to move goods overland, thereby avoiding the contrary winds and currents of the Dardanelles, and later as an exporter of stone for building.

But its greatest fame came in the middle of the fourth century BC when Assos was ruled by a student of Plato, Hermeias. Under Plato's guidance and with two of his disciples he sought to create an ideal city-state. A Platonic Academy was established and this attracted many of the most distinguished philosophers and scientists of the age, amongst them Aristotle and Theophrastus. These two carried out their early research in zoology, botany and biology at Assos, and may be called the fathers of these life sciences. Assos may have been to Aristotle what the Galapagos were to Darwin.

Below: The columns of the 6th century BC Temple of Athena at Assos.

Opposite: The harbour at Assos.

Hisarlik, the site of ancient Troy, may at first sight be a disappointment to some. Compared to the great sites further south, there is little grandeur to see. But go armed with Homer's Iliad well read, and the site will come alive.

Troy is strategically situated at the entrance to the narrows of the Dardanelles. At first it was probably a small fortified town (Troy I, 3500-3000 BC, and Troy II, 2800-2500 BC: there are nine distinct levels in all; with several sub-levels) engaged in minor trade and agriculture. In the second of these periods it was prosperous and the town was considerably enlarged. The treasure Schliemann found, which he thought was Priam's, came from this time. There was a significant setback at the end of this second period, with a great fire and invasion. The era 2200-1800 BC (levels III, IV and V) was not prosperous; the town shrank, and again the period ended with the destruction of the town and the settlement of new people who brought with them Bronze Age technology. Now Troy grew prosperous (level VI, 1800-1275 BC) on the export of Bronze Age products to the West. This was Priam's Troy, and the buildings and walls were well built and on a grander scale than before.

But Troy sat astride the main trade route to the Black Sea, and this probably led to the Trojan War, with the Achaean Greeks seeking to break through to exploit this trade. Alas, the city was ruined by a severe earthquake in 1275 BC. The next period (level VII, 1275 - 1100 BC) was one of decline, with poorer quality building and eventual takeover by a new Balkan people. A gap of four hundred years follows, until Troy became a Greek city (level VIII, 700 - 300 BC), with Xerxes and Alexander visiting it. A final prosperous period came next (level IX, 300 BC-300 AD), with Caesar offering sacrifices and Augustus new buildings. Constantine considered Troy as a possible site for his new capital in the east, but decided on Byzantium instead. Thereafter the decline to agricultural anonymity was gradual, with total disappearance coming by the 15th century AD.

Sit on the highest stone of the citadel at dusk, as the sun dips on the shore to the west, beyond the two mounds, the tumuli where Patroclus and Achilles are by legend said to be buried, and you will hear the ghosts of ancient warriors debating strategy. Troy will live forever, for it was the inspiration for the earliest European literature.

Below: The walls of ancient Troy.

Opposite: Replica Wooden Horse of Troy.

Above: Fisherman near Çanakkale, Europe opposite.

Above: Country family near Assos.

Unlike so many cities and towns of Turkey, Bursa played no significant part in ancient history. No doubt there was a settlement here from at least 1000 BC, for the site, on the verdant slopes of Ulu Dag, the Great Mountain, is too good to have been missed. Traditionally the town was founded by the Bithynian King Prusias on Hannibal's advice in the second century BC; and he named it Prusa, for himself.

Above: The approaches to Bursa (Allom and Walsh, 1838).

It is as the homeplace of the Ottomans that Bursa first became famous. Arabic script has no P, so the name changed. It fell to the Ottomans in 1326, and became their capital for nearly a century. But even after the capital of the expanding Ottoman Empire was transferred to Edirne, Bursa retained its eminence in the old Ottoman heartland. Osman Gazi, the founder of the Ottoman dynasty, is buried there, as are his five successor sultans.

Their lovely mosques, and the caravanserai which crowded round the former, perch on the foothills of the Great Mountain. This is a superb town to visit to taste the Ottoman imperial past, and it is at its best in spring, when the air is clear and the hills are green.

Below and opposite: The Emir Sultan Mosque complex at Bursa.

Across much of Turkey (and indeed Central Asia) hans or caravanserai were built so that merchants and travellers could be secure at night from attack by robbers. Typically a han was a large fortified courtyard, with many separate rooms facing the courtyard. The Seljuks and later the Ottomans were avid builders of such refuges, usually a day's journey from each other on the main trade routes. Today many, and especially those in the cities, are being renovated for use as shops.

Above: Restoration of a han completed.

Opposite: The restoration of a han in progress at Bursa.

Above: The busy courtyard of a han (Allom and Walsh, 1838).

Iznik has more than most prospered and suffered from the vicissitudes of history. Thrice the capital of kingdoms and once of an empire, it has been captured and recaptured by Goths, Persians, Mongols, Seljuks and Crusaders. The greatest catastrophes were in 1402, when Timur sacked the city, and in 1922 when the town was ravaged in the last days of the Greco-Turkish war.

Today the most impressive sight is the massive walls, which encompass an area considerably larger than the town itself. The walls in the main date from late Byzantine times, with modifications and repairs by both the Seljuks and the Ottomans.

The city was founded in 316 BC by Antigonus the One-Eyed, one of Alexander's generals, who ruled much of the centre of Alexander's disintegrated empire. Shortly afterwards it came under the rule of the King of Thrace, who named it Nicaea, after his deceased wife. The last King of Bithynia willed it to Rome, and it became an important city of the Eastern Roman Empire. Constantine, Diocletian and Justinian all lived here. The first Ecumenical Council of the Christian Church was convened in Nicaea by Constantine in 325; and there emerged the Nicaean Creed. The town was renamed Iznik in the 14th century.

Iznik's greatest claim to fame is its ceramics. It recovered quickly from the disaster of 1402, and for the next two centuries produced some of the finest ceramic work the world has seen. Many of the Ottoman mosques are decorated with its beautiful tiles (see pages 58-59).

Today the town is a pleasant market town, surrounded by massive walls which testify to its magnificent but chequered history.

Left: Storks nesting on Iznik's museum.

Opposite: The massive walls of Iznik.

BIBLIOGRAPHY

Akurgal, E.
"Ancient Civilizations and Ruins of Turkey", *Istanbul 1970*

Akurgal, E.
"The Art and Architecture of Turkey", *Oxford 1980*

Akurgal, E.
"The Hittites", March 1962

Alkim, U.B.
"Anatolia I", *Geneva 1969*

Allom J. and Walsh, R.
"Constantinople and the Seven Churches of Asia Minor", *London 1838*

Bartlett, W.H.
"Syria, The Holy Land and Asia Minor", *3 vols., London 1836.*

Bean, G.E.
"Aegean Turkey, An Archaeological Guide", *London 1966*

Bean, G.E.
"Lycian Turkey, An Archaeological Guide", *London 1978*

Bean, G.E.
"Turkey's Southern Shore", *London 1979*

Bean, G.E.
"Beyond the Meander", *London 1980*

Bradford, E.
"The Great Betrayal, Constantinople 1204", *London 1967*

Brossett, M.
"Ruines D'Ani", *St. Petersburg 1860*

Cahen, C.
"Pre-Ottoman Turkey", *London 1968*

Coles, P.
"The Ottoman Impact on Europe", *London 1968*

Cook, J.M.
"The Persian Empire", *London 1983*

Davison, R.H.
"Turkey, A Short History", *Beverley 1981*

Fellows, Charles.
"Discoveries in Lycia", *London 1841*

Fox, Robin Lane
"Alexander the Great", *London 1973*

Freely, J.
"Turkey", *London 1973*

Gibbons, H.A.
"The Foundation of the Ottoman Empire. A History of the Osmanlis, up to the Death of Bayezid I 1300-1403", *London 1968*

Goodwin, G.
"History of Ottoman Architecture", *London 1971*

Grousset, R.
"The Empire of the Steppes", *New Brunswick 1970*

Gurney, O.R.
"The Hittites", *London 1980*

Herodotus
"The Histories", *Penguin, London 1959*

Hill, D. and Grabor, O.
"Islamic Architecture", *London 1967*

Kinross, Lord
"Within the Taurus", *London 1954*

Kinross, Lord
"Atatürk. The Rebirth of a Nation", *London 1964*

Lang, D.M.
"Armenia", *London 1970*

Lewis, B.
"The Emergence of Modern Turkey", *London 1966*

Lewis, G.
"Turkey", *London 1965*

Lewis, R.
"Everyday Life in Ottoman Turkey", *London 1971).*

Lloyd, S.
"Early Anatolia", *London 1956*

Lloyd, S.
"Early Highland Peoples of Anatolia", *London 1967*

Lynch, H.F.B.
"Armenia", *2 vols., London 1901*

Macqueen, J.G.
"The Hittites and their Contemporaries in Asia Minor", *London 1986*

Mayer, L.
"Views in the Ottoman Empire", *London 1803*

Mellaart, J.
"Catal Huyuk. A Neolithic Town in Turkey", *London 1967*

Mellaart, J.
"The Archaeology of Ancient Turkey", *London 1978*

Metzger, H.
"Anatolia II", *Geneva 1969*

Miller, W.
"Trebizond, The Last Christian Empire", *London 1926*

Morier, J.
"A Journey Through Persia, Armenia and Asia Minor", *London 1812*

Morier, J.
"A Second Journey Through Persia, Armenia and Asia Minor", *London 1818*

Ostrogorsky, G.
"History of the Byzantine State", *Oxford 1956*

Pardoe, J. and Bartlett, W.H.
"Beauties of the Bosphorus", *London 1839*

Pereira, M.
"East of Trebizond", *London 1971*

Pitcher, D.E.
"An Historical Geography of the Ottoman Empire", *Leiden 1972*

Rice, D.T.
"The Byzantines", *London 1962*

Rice, T.T.
"The Seljuks in Asia Minor", *London 1961*

Rodley, L.
"Cave Monasteries of Byzantine Cappadocia", *Cambridge 1985*

Runciman, S.
"The Fall of Constantinople 1453", *Cambridge 1969*

Setton, K.M. and Baldwin M.W., eds.
"A History of the Crusades, Vol. 1, The First Hundred Years", *Wisconsin 1969*

Setton, K.M. Wolff, R.L. and Hazard, H.W.
"A History of the Crusades, Vol. 2, The Later Crusades 1189-1311", *Wisconsin 1975*

Setton, K.M. and Hazard, H.W.
"A History of the Crusades, Vol.3, The Fourteenth and Fifteenth Centuries", *Wisconsin 1975*

Shaw, S.J.,
"History of the Ottoman Empire and Modern Turkey. Vol. 1, The Empire of the Gazis", *Cambridge 1976*

Shaw, S.J. and Shaw, E.K.
"History of the Ottoman Empire and Modern Turkey, Vol. 2, Reform, Revolution and Republic", *Cambridge 1977*

Stark, F.
"Ionia", *London 1954*

Stark, F.
"The Lycian Shore", *London 1956*

Stark, F.
"Alexander's Path", *London 1958*

Stark, F.
"Riding to the Tigris", *London 1959*

Stark, F.
"Rome on the Euphrates", *London 1966*

Stark, F. and Roiter, F.
"Turkey", *London 1971*

Stratton, A.
"Sinan", *London 1972*

Stewart, C.
"Byzantine Legacy", *London 1974*

Sumner-Boyd, H. and Freely, J.
"Strolling Through Istanbul", *London 1972*

Warkworth, Lord
"Asiatic Turkey", *London 1898*

Williams, G.
"Turkey. A Traveller's Guide and History", *London 1967*

"Williams, G.
"Eastern Turkey", *London 1972*